DAKOTA DIASPORA

Memoirs of a Jewish Homesteader

by Sophie Trupin

ALTERNATIVE PRESS

Cover design and illustration by Brian Groppe.
Book design by Anne Moose.
Printing by Edwards Brothers Inc.

ISBN: 0-9606346-3-0 (paperback)
ISBN: 0-9606346-4-9 (hardcover)

Alternative Press
P.O. Box 4798
Berkeley, California 94704

10   9   8   7   6   5   4   3   2

Printed in the United States of America.

The following pages are dedicated to the memory of my parents, Gittel and Harry Turnoy, and their neighbors, who braved the unknown and unfamiliar in search of a life with dignity; and to my children, whose lives, though different, retain the values—ethical and spiritual—that link them with their grandparents and with their Jewish heritage.

Acknowledgements

Thank you Dan, my husband and companion for the greater part of my life, for reading aloud to me all these many years. Your reading these vignettes in such an engaging manner gave me the confidence to allow the strangers who open this book to share my thoughts.

Friends and relatives have also been of much help in their encouragement and support. I wish to thank my children, Robert and Joella, and my grandchildren, Naomi, Theresa, Reevan, Gabriel and Johanna, who were the inspiration that prompted me to delve into my past. I extend special thanks to Annie Moose, who is my publisher and much much more. Her confidence, youthful enthusiasm and warmth have allayed some of my timidity and reluctance to venture forth into the world of letters.

The following people have been tremendously helpful in various ways, and I appreciate them all. Many thanks to Edith Atkin, Jeanne Dritz, Doctor Harold Eiser, Reuven Goldfarb, Lillian Heyman, Jeffrey Kessel, Frances Koestler, Gladys Leider, Rose Lerman, Kenneth Libo, Rosalyn Moss, David Moss, Ruth Polsky, Barbara Riddle, Rebecca Shallit, Bernard Shallit, William Shorr, Stan Sikorski, Gene Trupin, Lenny Trupin, Gerry Turnoy, Sue Turnoy, and Esther Waning.

Table of Contents

Introduction   *1*

The Old Country
Counterattack   5
See the Drunken Gentiles   7
My Father and Mother   9

My Father in the New World
Father in Chicago   15
The Lonely Years   17

The Journey
Little Grandmother   23
Crossing the Atlantic   25
The Journey Continued   28
The Arrival   31

Trapped in a Strange Land
Worlds Apart   35
The Harvest   36
Two Worlds   39
Stranger   41
The Pollack House   43
Revelation   46

A New Life
School Days   51
First Generation American   53
Yiddishe Mamma   55
The Knipple   57

Food   59
Siblings   61
The Mikvah   63

Jews and Gentiles

Neighbors   69
Rabbi Hess   70
Keeping House   72
The Party   73
The Melting Pot   75
Separateness   77

Winter

Snowbound   81
The Blizzard   82
Charlie   84

Holy Days

Spring and Passover   89
Heritage and Tradition   91
The Double Wedding   95

A Town is Born

Wing, North Dakota   101
Civilization   102
The Fourth of July   105
August 1914   107
The Peddler   109
Reading and Writing   112
Camille   113
Brief Encounter   115
Beautiful Dreamer   118

The War Years

1917   125
My Friend   127
Wartime Harvest   128
My Teacher   133
Graduation Day   135

Remembering

Vanished Past   141
The Gingham Dress   142
Chokecherries on the Hill   144

Years Later

Only Human   149
The Black Years   150
Strangers No Longer   151
Israel   152

DAKOTA DIASPORA
Memoirs of a Jewish Homesteader

Introduction

When I think about the Jewish settlers in North Dakota at the turn of the century, I often despair of ever being able to put down on paper the chronicle of that small band of adventurers. The word *adventurers* seems so incongruous to describe these earnest, simple people, and yet how else can I speak of them?

To most immigrants, that is, Jewish immigrants, New York was America; some would dare venture as far as Chicago. They continued the trades they brought with them; they labored in sweatshops, peddled, or worked themselves up to the luxurious affluence of sweating it out seven days weekly in their own little candy or grocery stores. It was better than the Old Country, but not too different. They heard the same language, smelled the same musty odors in their synagogues. The rest of America was there, somewhere, but they knew and cared little about it.

But the Jewish immigrants who settled in the wilderness of North Dakota were different; they were a special breed. Each was a Moses in his own right, leading his people out of the land of bondage—out of czarist Russia, out of anti-Semitic Poland, out of Roumania and Galicia. Each was leading his family to a promised land; only this was no land flowing with milk and honey—no land of olive trees and vineyards.

This was a harsh, forbidding land, which had lain untouched by human toil since the beginning of time. Only the prairie winds had roamed this empty space. The ground was there—good black soil beneath the prairie grass—but before it could be cultivated it had to be cleared. Before you could set plow to furrow you had to remove the rocks that strewed every foot of this land—rocks of every size and shape. What toil, what zeal and determination went into the clearing of each acre, reclaiming the land from its primitive state and cultivating it to yield food for sustenance. It seems to me, as I look back, that all the rows and heaps of rocks that lay along each cleared field were stained with the sweat of these zealots.

What did it matter if the work was backbreaking, if the winters were severe and endless? The harsh winds of the prairies in winter were less bitter than the winds of oppression, hatred and intolerance that had buffeted them in Europe.

In North Dakota they were at the mercy of nature. Their livelihood depended upon whether the rains came in time and the frosts not too soon. It depended on whether or not a prairie fire, fanned by the autumn winds and carried along by the tumbleweeds which served as flaming torches, would consume the crops standing in stacks waiting for the thrashing machine. Fire might even destroy the house that you and your family had labored on.

Yes, it all could, and often did, happen. And yet it was nothing compared to the cruelty of man against man. It was still nature's caprice, not man's calculated cruelty. There would always be another spring, another rainfall, another sowing, and another harvesting.

The Old Country

Counterattack

People often wondered what prompted my father to embark on a life so foreign to his people and to his training. There must have been an accumulation of experiences during my father's life in the Old Country that made him dissatisfied with existence there and anxious to try a new life in America. I know of a couple of such experiences, for I heard them described more than once. This one remains in my mind an unforgettable story.

It was the Sabbath and my father was in the synagogue praying. About him were the men of the congregation, all wrapped in their prayer shawls, intoning the ancient melodies, rocking gently to and fro. Suddenly there was a crash of broken glass, which made every head jerk up in alarm.

A heavy rock had been thrown through the small, unadorned window of the *shul*, interrupting the ancient Sabbath prayers. Some drunken peasants were having sport with the Jews. The rabbi looked helplessly at his congregation, then raised his eyes pleadingly to God in Heaven. Another rock came hurtling through another window, and wild, drunken laughter and derisive jeers and oaths broke the hush of the assembled worshipers. Soon the door would be pushed open. Coarse, unclean hands would hurl the sacred books into the bearded faces of the terrified Jews.

My father sprang into action. "Come, let's rip up the benches and defend ourselves."

The rabbi and the older men were horrified; to break the Sabbath by any physical work was a sin. My father answered that these drunken *muzhiks* knew this and were taking advantage of them when they were the most helpless. Surely God would understand that the only language these heathens knew was the language of force. The congregation must respond in kind. In response to my father the young men started ripping up the wooden benches, while the rabbi began to pray in such earnest desperation that the older men felt that God could do no less than heed his pleas.

The door was pushed open and the mob of violent anti-Semites poured in. But the younger men were ready for them with planks of wood and anything else at their disposal. Never had these ruffians encountered such a sight. Resistance on the Sabbath was unknown. Always the Jews had continued to pray even more loudly, wrapped in their prayer shawls, tears streaming down their faces, never lifting their eyes, except to God, until the synagogue lay in shambles. This was something new—something strange and unexpected. These young Jews were not praying; they were cursing in the Russian the mob understood, and counterattacking with all their strength.

The enemy retreated with a few bruises, shaking their bleeding, bewildered heads. In the synagogue the praying continued, the congregation standing, for the benches had been broken and put to a strange use. They all stood a little taller, and their voices were raised in thankfulness to God, who had delivered them once more.

When my father came home from *shul* that afternoon and kissed the *mezuzah* on the frame of the doorway leading into our home, he saw it very clearly. He would not remain in this land of persecution and oppression. He was still young and strong; he would go to America. He knew exactly what he would do. He would be a farmer, a homesteader. He had read in the Yiddish newspaper, published in some large city in Russia, that there was a movement afoot to help Jewish immigrants from anti-Semitic countries of Europe to settle on free government land in the New World. There was an organization of Jewish philanthropists in America that would lend money to any Jew who wished to emigrate to an uninhabited part of the United States.

The idea of going to America was born in my father's mind that day. It needed only one more experience to turn the idea into a resolution.

See the Drunken Gentiles

When my little brother was four or five years old, he used to listen to stories of the Old Country and the voyage. Every time he heard them he would interject, "Oh yes, I remember being on that ship." We would laugh and nod indulgently, "Of course you remember."

Now I find myself in much the same situation. There is one incident which I can describe which occurred when I was about a year and a half old. I am in a strange room where I have never been before. With me are my family— my brothers, sister, father and mother—and I don't know who else. It is all very vague, except for the feeling of strangeness. I am not scared, just interested. There seems to be a small window through which the light of day comes, and I can hear the sound of harsh voices like a roar.

My mother used to tell me that we had taken shelter in the attic of the house we lived in because a *pogrom* was raging in our town, and we were hiding from the mob. She told me that she had lifted me, at my insistence, to look out onto the street, and that I had said in my baby talk in Yiddish, "*Zeh di shitere doyam*," which in real Yiddish should be, "*Zeh di shikere goyim*." Translated, it means, "See the drunken Gentiles."

A while ago my eldest brother, who was nine at the time of this *pogrom*, told me that it was on the occasion of this half-remembered scene that our father decided to come to this country. My brother described the scene in the attic and filled in all the details. He told me that my father at that time was in the cheese business. He would buy tremendous round cheeses, the size of small table tops, and with a very long knife cut them into pieces to sell. On the day of the *pogrom*, when our town was invaded by a crowd of bloodthirsty Russians, my father and mother and we four children took refuge in the attic, hoping that we would not be discovered. My father had his long cheese knife. He decided that before he and his family were killed he would kill as many of the attackers as he possibly could. It was up in that attic, surrounded by his terrified family, that my father vowed that he would leave this accursed Russia and make a new life for himself and his family in America.

My brother told me that what really saved us that day was the quick wit of our Gentile landlord. Upon hearing the mob approaching, he came out of his house and stood outside the gate. He waved his hand in a friendly salute and as they neared the house said something to ward them off. "Don't waste your time here, my brothers; I wouldn't have those Jew dogs in my house."

And so the mob by-passed our house and we continued to live.

We are here today, those of us who are still alive, because my father kept the vow he made as he waited like a trapped animal, helpless and impotent, not knowing if he would survive to carry out his pledge. The others of my father's and mother's families were not so fortunate. Forty years later, when the Nazi hordes marched through Europe, they found our little town and slaughtered and gassed almost every member of our family. Only two cousins, the daughters of my mother's brother, managed to hide and escape. After many years of wandering and hardship and separation, they finally met in the land of Israel.

My Father and Mother

My father had certainly not been trained to be a farmer. He had been a *yeshiva* boy, a student of the Torah when he was growing up in the Old Country. My father's studies began when he was five years old and he was sent to the *cheder*. Later he was sent to the *yeshiva*. That meant studying the Torah from the moment it got light until dusk, or even later by candlelight. He was the first-born son, and on him rested the responsibility of carrying on the tradition of his family and his people. When my father left the *yeshiva* he worked for a man who was a *Hasid*. He admired this man and his way of life, and considered joining the *Hasidim*. Eventually, however, he decided to remain as he had been reared.

When he entered adult life, my father went into the cheese importing business. He learned a lot in this business,

and I remember the various cheeses he used to make on
the farm after we moved to America. But most of all he
was a student—a student of the interpretations and fine
points of the Law.

My father was not a giant. He was of medium height,
and broad-shouldered. His walk was definite and solid, as
though he knew every moment where he was headed for.
In spite of the backbreaking work, his back remained
straight, his head erect, his sharp blue eyes direct and uncompromising. I never remember my father dragging his
feet or seeming weary. When fatigue overtook him he
would lie down and sleep for a while, then arise completely
refreshed.

In all his dealings he was scrupulously honest, and he
could find no possible excuse for anyone being otherwise.
There was no shortcut to honesty; it went all the way. Your
landlord might be a millionaire, and you might not be able
to pay the rent, but you were committed to pay him back
when you found a job and saved up the rent due. My
father, and people like him, would disapprove vehemently
of the common practice today of even little thefts, like
taking home some stationery from the office or trying to
get away without paying for a phone call. Since money had
never tempted him, he could not understand or condone
such weaknesses in others.

The Ten Commandments—all of them—were not
something my father took lightly. He lived by them every
day of his life. To live in this prescribed way did not seem
unusual or noble. To do otherwise was unthinkable. Today
his sense of morality seems almost archaic.

It seemed that my father's nature, like that of many
people, was made up of contradictory feelings. He was

proud of his Jewish heritage, yet very critical of his fellow Jews. Somehow they must set an example. They must be beyond reproach in every phase of their lives. If one Jew was dishonest, or failed to live up to the highest moral standards, then all Jews must bear the shame of such an individual. It was carrying the honor system to its ultimate. This attitude was not rare among the Jews of my father's generation, and even those who came later.

My mother's life in the Old Country had been fairly sheltered. One could sense that just from her appearance. I can best describe her from a photograph taken with her two brothers in the Old Country. Her brothers were both living in Warsaw and wore moustaches and clothes of that period. My mother was seated with her brothers to the left of her. She sat very straight, with her head held high, or so it appeared because of the collar of lace which reached up under her chin and behind her ears, probably held up by a thin wire frame. Her waist was small, and her figure graceful and feminine. Her hands were folded in her lap, and her sleeves fit snugly from the elbow to the wrist, and were quite full from the elbow to the shoulders. Her hair was brushed up and twisted into a bun on top of her head. Her face was serene and gentle, and belied the haughty pose.

My mother was considered delicate, though she was not a sick person. She was pampered, perhaps, being the only daughter of a doting mother. In the summertime she was sent to breathe the invigorating air of a *dachta*, or country place. It was equivalent to going to a summer resort. There was always a housemaid to do the heavy work, and when my mother's third child was born, a wet nurse was employed to feed him. She was as unprepared for the life of a pioneer woman as she could possibly be, and had she known what awaited her in "Nordokota," or North Dakota, as I learned to pronounce it, I doubt that she would ever have taken that journey.

Years later I met my father's sister, who had known my mother as a young girl when she was being courted by my father. My aunt told me that my mother was the prettiest girl in the village. Although my father and she were cousins, they had never met until they were both grown-ups, and then it was love at first sight. In those days marriages were arranged by the parents through a *shadchan*, or matchmaker. It was seldom that young people took matters into their own hands, but my father and mother were an exception. I can't imagine my father being told whom to marry.

My Father in the
New World

Father in Chicago

I have pieced together bit by bit how Father fared in the intervening years between the time he left the Old Country and the day his family arrived to join him. I remember him telling of his arrival and stopover in Chicago, where his younger brother had emigrated several years before.

Perhaps *emigrated* is not quite the word. *Escaped to* would be more accurate, for my uncle was slated to be conscripted into the army of the czar. My uncle was a Talmudist, a *yeshiva* boy, a mild-mannered, peaceful young man. He had no stomach for the life of a soldier, so he ran away to America. I don't know just how he managed it, but there he was in this growing, sprawling city of Chicago, living in the Jewish section of Maxwell Street, making a living as a peddler.

When my father arrived, my uncle tried to impress on his older and more dynamic brother that fortune awaited him in this city. Why should he travel so far from civilization to embark on an arduous and uncertain venture? Homesteading and farming were not for Jews, steeped in learning, knowing only commerce, trade, and skills. He painted a glowing picture of the goals they could reach working together, but my father was unimpressed. He had not come to this country to be a merchant. He had left his family and his homeland for nobler purposes. Too long had Jews been identified with trading and dealing. Somehow, my father felt it necessary to change that image. To win the respect of the Christian world, Jews must work with their hands—not in shops and factories, but on the land, producing food. Making money, getting rich—that was not important to my father. He had never been rich, but he had always provided a decent living for his family. He would continue to do so as long as he had the strength to work, but it would be in his own way.

My uncle pleaded with him to at least give himself a chance before he left for the new life he was embarking on. My father was impatient to be off, but his brother was so insistent that he postponed his departure for a day or two. He took a suitcase filled with ladies' shirtwaists that my uncle handed to him, and went out to peddle. I can visualize it all: Father dressed in his European clothes, knowing but a few words in English, yet unabashed and indifferent to the whole thing. I can see him knocking on doors, the housewives letting him stand there with the suitcase in his hand, and his polite, straightforward approach, neither humble nor brash.

After several hours of walking through the unfamiliar city streets, my father returned to his brother's house, put down the empty suitcase, and plunked the money on the table. My uncle looked at him in amazement. It had taken Father such a short time to dispose of the merchandise. He was a born salesman, a genius. His brother started to explain excitedly how, by virtue of this experiment, wealth lay within his grasp. He took a paper and pencil and figured out how much Father had earned that day by deducting the price Uncle had paid to the jobber for the blouses from the amount my father had received. In a few years they could save enough money to start a store, and soon, maybe, a department store could be theirs. My father was completely unmoved and uninterested.

"Brother," he said, "I only went through with this because you insisted. If I had brought back this suitcase full of gold, I would still not remain in this city or any other city. Be well and prosper. I have work to do. Tomorrow I shall be on a train headed for the West."

The Lonely Years

After Father filed his claim on the quarter section of land, and it was duly recorded in the county court, he set about making this claim valid. The government gave to each adult who applied one quarter section of virgin land, nothing more, with the proviso that one must live on it, improve it, and make it productive. If you lived up to this agreement, the land became yours after five years. Then it was yours to do with as you pleased. You could leave it, rent it, sell it, or continue to live on it without further improving it.

Father built a crude shack from whatever bits and pieces of scrap material he could find. Then he started to dig a well and build a fence. When winter came and the land lay locked and frozen, farming and building came to a halt, and my father went to the nearest coal mine and got a job in the coal pit. This kind of work was unknown to my father, and that is precisely why he did it. Just as he had to prove that a Jew could be a farmer to win the respect of the Christian world, he also believed that he must do whatever hard work was at hand, so long as it was honest toil. And so it was that here was a "sheeny" working alongside the "Polacks," the "wops," and the "Swedes."

During this period he also worked for the railroad as a tender, carrying water to the steam engines on the freezing winter nights. But at the first sign of spring, Father was back on the land, working feverishly from daybreak until dark. It must have been his Talmudic mind that stood him in such good stead. He had never been a carpenter, yet here he was building a home. He had never built a fence, yet he was building his own, and instructing the other home-steaders who were also novices. He had no money for lumber, and there were no trees anywhere in the whole vast area. There were a few railroad ties which were charred and unfit for use on the track, and he managed to lug them back from the station depot where he had been working. These served as the framework for the house and barn. With a plow he cut squares of earth held together by the grass which grew from them, and from these he made the roof. This earth is called *sod*; hence, the name *sod house*. The floor was made of rough boards which had been discarded by neighbors. It was weather-beaten and splintered. I should know, for I often scrubbed that floor when I was a little girl.

My father also planted a garden, and cleared the fields. The days were never long enough for all there was to do. When it was too dark to work out of doors, he set the dough to rise and kneaded it into loaves to bake the following morning. One must have nourishment to gather the strength to work as hard as he did.

I used to wonder and marvel at the fortitude with which my father passed the long, lonely years until his family joined him in this new land. I remember my father always singing, no matter what his mood. Perhaps this was the secret to his successful struggle against loneliness when he was isolated on that vast sea of prairie.

I recall the first time I ever heard an American song. It was Father singing "In the Shade the Old Apple Tree." Another song was "Pretty Little Red Wing." They were new to me and yet not so new, for everything he sang had a bit of the old Hebraic flavor of the endless liturgical intoning that he had known and loved since his boyhood days in the *yeshiva*.

My father also spoke to the animals. They were his friends. He had much more than the cloying love some people have for animals. He had respect for them. Without his cows there would be no milk and cheese and butter. Without the chickens there would be no eggs. Without his horses there would be no plowing and haying and harvesting.

My oldest brother described to me once what a neighbor had told him about our father before we came to join him. It happened a year before our arrival. Father had put in a crop that spring with his one horse and mule. The rains had come in time; the sun had shone at the right times. The hail had stayed away, and so had the grasshoppers. The wheat and oats had ripened. He had reaped a good harvest. The wheat was ready for thrashing when a spark from the thrashing machine set the stacks of wheat on fire. All the year's toil turned to ashes, and with it my father's hope that his family would join him that year. The money for their journey would now have to come from the next year's crop.

This neighbor told my brother how my father had mounted his horse and, with tears blinding him, ridden away. Hours later he returned to the heaps of ashes that had been his crop. Next spring he would start again, plant his fields, and hope and pray for another harvest.

The Journey

Little Grandmother

W hen my father left us behind in the Old Country it was 1904, and I was less than two years old. My mother and we four children remained in Russia and went to live with my grandmother, my mother's mother, in the little village of Seltz.

I remember my grandmother quite well, both from having lived with her and from a photograph my mother used to look at, wiping away the tears as she did so. My grandmother was small, fragile, and very devout. She wore a black silk dress and a *sheitel*, or wig, of straight black hair over which she wore a black wool shawl. She was a widow and made her living by running a little dry goods store. She arose before dawn every day of the week, put up the *samovar* with charcoal and water, and went out to purchase fresh bagels and *halvah*, which she left on the dining room table. Before opening her store, she went to *shul* to pray. Hours later, we awoke to breakfast. My two brothers went off to *cheder*, and my sister and I played with out friends while my mother busied herself with the light chores. Three times a week my grandmother fasted. Also, once a week she prepared a basket of food for some poor family who otherwise would have little with which to usher in the Sabbath. Her life was devoted to work, prayer, and charity.

Life in that little Russian village ghetto was very sheltered and peaceful. People expected very little. Every thought and action was geared towards insuring a good place in the hereafter. The Jews spoke of *der emeseh velt*, the true world. It was here that good Jews went after they left this false life which was just a painful interlude through which they passed with bowed heads, humble prayers, and strict obedience to God's commands. I can understand how my father could never resign himself to such a life. He could bow his head to God, but he believed in himself and in the dignity of man. When he left the Old Country, he was seeking a life which had value, meaning, and dignity on this earth.

I remember the long winter afternoons in the warm kitchen of my mother's good friend, where the young wives gathered to gossip and make feather pillows. At one end of the kitchen was the *pripetshik*, or oven, which was used for heating as well as cooking. Every table and bench was covered with goose feathers, and every woman and big girl and little girl was busy stripping the fine feathers from the stems and stuffing them into pillowcases. The whole room was seen through a haze of fine down, which floated and settled on everything. Every mother who had daughters had the task of providing each one with several huge pillows and *perenehs*, or quilts, filled with goose feathers and down. And that was no easy task.

I also remember that certain Sundays were different from other days; they must have been market days. The peasants would come into the village to purchase things. I remember my sister and I sitting on low stools in front of grandmother's little store with a large assortment of frilly bonnets in a basket beside us. The peasant women would try the bonnets on us to see which ones they wished to buy for their little girls. I enjoyed being a model, for I loved being told how pretty I looked.

Had we remained in the little village, perhaps my memory would not go back so far or so vividly. The days would run into each other and become a blur. But so much began to happen all at once. We began to make preparations for our departure for America—all those pretty flowered fabrics from my grandmother's store being sewn into dresses for my sister and me, those shiny new shoes, and, what I loved best of all, a velvet coat of pale blue and white, as fleecy as a cloud on a summer's day. I was so excited and happy about the whole thing that it never occurred to me that sadness accompanies departures. I do remember the very last evening in my grandmother's house when every room was filled with friends who had come to bid us farewell and safe crossing. I felt so important showing my new wardrobe to my admiring playmates. But, somehow, I must have sensed a little of the sadness which my grandmother tried to hide. She kept stroking my head and saying, "My little songbird is flying away."

And now, after all these years—so many, many years—I recall the scene, and I shed the tears I failed to shed as a very excited little girl. I never saw my grandmother again, for she remained in the Old Country. Twenty years later, when I was pregnant with my first child, my mother wrote to me that my grandmother had passed away in the little village where her friends had cared for her in her last years.

Crossing the Atlantic

Four years after my father left for America, my mother and we four children finally crossed the Atlantic. It was a time when immigration was perhaps at its highest point in history. Anything that floated was pressed into service. I have my mother's passport, and the date is July, 1908.

The voyage to America seemed endless, and the world of water that engulfed us was terrifying. We spent most of our time below deck in what must have been the steerage section. It was a dimly lit, low ceilinged room, quite large and round, with bunks built into the walls. Each family occupied a section of upper and lower bunks.

The galley and dining room were on a raised platform; at one end there was a huge table with benches around it. I don't remember any of the adults ever partaking of the food served here; perhaps it was because it was not considered kosher. Their main fare consisted of *suchares*, or dehydrated bread, which each family had prepared before departure. Such bread withstood mold and could sustain life. Each morning one of us, whoever happened to be the least sick, went on deck to purchase oranges and bars of chocolate.

I believe the children under thirteen had special dispensation, and could eat the food served at the table without breaking the dietary laws. I remember tasting soup at that table and being very disappointed; it seemed to have sugar in it. I thought to myself, "What heathens, to put sugar in soup." Whatever I tasted at that table seemed too sweet, so I seldom bothered to eat there. Perhaps the food tasted sweet to me because of the bitter taste in my mouth from the perpetual vomiting due to seasickness. That tub of a ship was tossed about mercilessly by the huge waves.

I recall how annoyed I got whenever I saw the kitchen help, dressed in their white aprons and chef's hats, tossing the garbage through the portholes into the sea. Didn't they realize that by dumping all that stuff into the water they were making the ocean even higher and more dangerous? It was much too deep already. I can't understand how my child's mind reasoned it all out, but that was how I felt, and it seemed very logical to me.

I have no recollection of playing with children on the ship, though there must have been many on board. I suppose we were all too sick and weary.

I do remember Ellis Island. I have a picture in my mind of a room with a rocking chair in it. I had never seen such a chair, and I enjoyed rocking in it. The other children liked it too, and we took turns sitting in it. I also remember night time, and the lights of the city across from us. It must have been summertime, for we were sitting on steps out of doors—a group of children my own age—and we were singing. I recall one of those songs. It was *"Kum Yisrael, kum aheym"*—"Come Israel, come home." I didn't understand its significance; I thought it was just about a little boy who had wandered away from home, whose mother was calling him back. But there was something so sad and haunting about it that I remember only that song, though we sang many more. Or perhaps even at six a Jewish child knows instinctively the longing for a home, and the ceaseless wanderings of the homeless Jews.

A child lives only in the moment, without nostalgia for the past or thought of the future. Surely I did not feel what my mother and the other adults must have experienced—to leave all that was familiar and dear. To be rejected and despised by the land that gave them birth; to brave the unknown; to find a strange land, a strange tongue, a strange people. And, added to this, to be without money, for they were poor people. But they did not come with empty hands. They brought with them a culture as old as civilization itself. They asked only for the right to work, to breathe the air of a free country, and to serve with dignity.

The Journey Continued

After the long voyage across the ocean the journey began all over again, but this time along endless miles of railroad tracks. Somewhere in this vast country was a place called "Nordokota." I had heard that strange name again and again for as long as I could remember. That was where our traveling would come to an end. We had no idea what it would be like. But, whatever it was, we would finally rest.

I remember the scratchy, plush seats of those grimy trains, and the perpetual jolting and jostling. I can still feel the weariness I felt as I tried to sleep, but was kept awake by sudden jolts, and by lights always there in the ceiling. If only there was some peaceful darkness; if only I could be on some stationary, motionless bed with the gentle night surrounding me.

We came to a place called Chicago, and my uncle came to the depot to meet us. He brought us a basket filled with fresh fruit. There were apples and oranges and some strange, long yellow fruits which I had never seen before. My uncle said they were bananas, and good to eat. I tasted one, and it had an odd taste. It wasn't juicy or crisp or sour; it just wasn't anything, but my uncle said it was good.

Next he took us to a large store where there were many different things. He bought my sister and me lovely hats made of cream-colored straw and covered with flowers.

In America little girls did not wear shawls. We walked out of the store wearing those beautiful hats, and at once we became Americans.

Our uncle then took us to his home, where his wife prepared food for us. As we entered the apartment we were greeted with the aroma of *gefilte fish*, and the pungent odor of cooking onions. On the table was a huge *challah*, freshly baked and glistening with the luster made by brushing beaten egg yolk over it before baking. For the first time since we left the Old Country, we were sitting down to a traditional meal with the Sabbath candles lit, the blessing of the wine, and people from our own family around us.

Then we were traveling westward once more. We must have presented a strange picture with our foreign clothes and battered baggage. I imagine we appeared almost like a tableau, titled "A Jewish Immigrant Mother and Her Children": the central figure, a young, slight woman with a shawl draped across her shoulders; two young boys with caps and *peyes*, or earlocks, standing beside her; and two little girls in front with bundles at their feet. We spoke no English.

At last there came a day when we stepped off the train for the last time. I remember my oldest brother lifting my sister down from the platform. I remember it because although she was older than I by a year and a half, no one had to lift me off. I felt quite superior. My sister was not as robust as I, and the long journey had been more difficult for her.

At the depot we were met by the German-speaking family with whom we would stay until my father came to meet us. But we had arrived; this was the place—the address written on the return envelopes we received from my father: Wilton, Burleigh County, North Dakota, U.S.A.

At the home of this German family there was a little girl about my age. But what I recall more distinctly than the little girl is the doll which she kindly allowed me to play with. It was the first American doll I had ever seen, and it won my heart completely. It had blonde curls and blue eyes that opened and shut. Long lashes rested on her pink cheeks, her red lips parted in a sweet half smile, and she was dressed like a fairy princess, with lace edging on her petticoat and white shoes and little white socks. I could hardly breathe with the ecstasy I felt as I beheld the beauty of that perfect creature.

I loved the doll with all my heart, and wanted it with all the desperation of the very young, but my mother explained to me very patiently that the doll did not belong to me, and that she could not buy me such a doll. I remember weeping bitterly.

My mother no doubt told me what every mother tells her child. "Why are you so unreasonable? I just explained to you that you can't have this doll. It belongs to the little girl who let you play with it. You have your own doll in your baggage." My little Russian doll, with its porcelain head and painted-on hair, seemed all right before I had seen this lovely vision, but now it would never be the same.

The next scene that comes to mind is a darkening room and kerosene lamps being lit. We were sitting in the living room where the beautiful doll made her home. It was twilight. There were shadows in the corners, and there was still some light coming in through the windows.

Suddenly, there was a knock on the door and my father came in. The first recollection I have of him is that of a strange man, with a bronzed, weatherbeaten face, dressed in strange clothes, with tears streaming down his face, embracing my mother. I remember feeling startled. I was amazed by my mother's display of emotion towards this strange man—my father.

The Arrival

I remember the morning when we started on the last lap of our journey to the home my father had built for us. Wilton, where we had made our first stop in North Dakota, was twenty-five miles from my father's farm. Twenty-five miles today seems like just around the corner, but in 1908, on a rutted prairie road, over hills of varying sizes, with a wagon and a pair of horses, it took from sunup until dark to cover. My mother sat with my father on the bench that ran across the front of the wagon, and we children sat in the wagon box amidst the baggage and provisions.

I remember looking out upon the endless prairies. The road that stretched ahead was made by the wheels of wagons such as my father's, driven infrequently by the few farmers scattered over many miles. It ran through the steel gray grass that covered the rolling hills and valleys. There was hardly a quarter mile of level ground. The hills rolled on, one after the other—all sizes, all shapes, all heights. Some hills seemed so tall that we wondered how we could make it safely down the steep descent. The horses strained to reach the top, and then my father held the reins tightly to keep them from galloping too quickly down the incline.

We traveled all day, and I don't remember meeting any other wagon or stopping anywhere. There were no houses or trees or rivers, only prairies and hills and sky. It was all strange and awesome, but very interesting to me. To my mother it must have been fearsome and devastating to be plunged into this vast, empty world after knowing only the narrow confines of her familiar ghetto. Here there were no towns, no *shuls*, no *Talmud Torahs* where her sons might continue to learn, no *kashruth*, no *yiddishkeit*. This was an alien, heathen land, harsh and bare and hostile.

Finally, we saw the farm. The wheat had been harvested and stood in stacks waiting to be thrashed. The fields were shorn but not yet bare. Along each field lay piles of rocks in heaps; each rock had been dug out of the surface of the earth and carried or rolled to make these heaps. The cleared fields seemed to be swallowed up in the vast land that stretched endlessly in all directions. As we drove up the slope of the low hill and into the yard, we saw the barn and the house.

It was dusk when we entered the house my father had built. A kerosene lamp was lit. I have a recollection of dark shadows and an iron bed, its head a metal curlicue. I slept in this bed that first night. I suppose it was too late to make up a separate place for me. Since I was the youngest, it must have seemed all right to put me at the foot of my parents' bed. But to me it seemed odd and unpleasant to sleep in a bed where my mother was with a strange man. Yes, he was my father, but still a stranger.

Trapped in a Strange Land

Worlds Apart

It was always a mystery to me how two people with a common background, who had married for love, who had five children, who had lived together harmoniously for a number of years, and had corresponded for four years, could have known so little about one another's needs. Although my parents trod the same ground, felt the same wind in their faces, and looked upon the same hills and valleys, they each saw something completely different.

My father saw a promised land free from anti-Semitism and degradation. This piece of land, rock-strewn and stubborn, was his and would be a legacy to his children. In the Old Country he could not own even one acre because he was a Jew. Here he was not only a Jew; he was a man, and could live in dignity. This life was a challenge and he met it; he had the physical strength to do so, and the certainty that he was doing what was best for himself and his family. My father had written often to my mother about the new life he was building for her and the children. In his letters to her he must have conveyed these confident assurances, and for him it was the truth.

Yet, when my mother finally arrived, she was dismayed and horrified at what she found. She saw a sod house with a rough, splintered floor, a crude homemade table with two benches which my father had fashioned from planks, iron bedsteads with sagging springs, and a blackened kitchen range. The well was in the valley at the foot of the hill upon which our house stood.

My father could not understand her reaction. He took such pride in his cleared fields and house and barn. He had thought his wife would be so proud of him! She would kiss every corner. This had been his envisioning, but instead his wife wrung her hands and wept. She felt trapped, betrayed, helpless. We were all trapped in this desolate land. My mother wept; my father stormed and raged. And there was work—hard, endless work.

The Harvest

My mother and we children were witnessing our first harvest on the homestead. We had been in this country only a few weeks and were learning, along with English, many new and strange ways.

The thrashing machine made its way from one farmer to the next, bringing with it a dozen or so hungry men. While the giant machine swallowed the bundles of wheat which were tossed into it—seeming to devour them, but merely separating the kernels from the chaff—the men would come to the table ready to devour mountains of home-cooked food.

My mother was initiated into the ritual of feeding the thrashers. Mrs. Pollack, Mrs. Edelberg, and Mrs. Luper were our closest neighbors, and were also Jewish home-steaders. They had arrived before my mother, and they came over to our house the day before the thrashing started to help and advise her.

The table must be set the night before for the morning breakfast, for at sunrise the men would enter the house. Most of these men were farmers who helped one another by exchanging services during the harvest period. There were also three or four men who were followers of the thrashing machine; they were I.W.W. men—Industrial Workers of the World—nicknamed Wobblies. They were, I believe, the first unionized men in this part of the country, and were considered socialistic because they demanded good food and a fair day's pay for a day's work. The prevailing wages were about three or four dollars a day, which was considered a great deal of money in comparison with what the farmers themselves earned.

The crew, dressed in their blue overalls and faded denim jackets, would all file into the house, settle themselves at the table, and get down to the business of consuming the enormous platters of food which my mother, my sister and I kept bringing from the kitchen range. There were piles of pancakes, bowls of oatmeal served with heavy sweet cream, dozens of sunny-side eggs fried in butter, heaps of home fried potatoes, loaves of homemade bread, coffeecakes, cheese blintzes, pitchers of milk, and gallons of coffee, freshly ground in the hand-turned mill. To eat like a thrasher was a byword for having a tremendous appetite.

No sooner had the men all piled out of the house than the preparations began for the midday meal, which was called *dinner*. This consisted of a huge pot roast with potatoes browned in gravy, bean and barley soup or whole yellow pea soup made with beef and mushrooms, pickles, sauerkraut, beets, carrots, more milk and more coffee, and, most important of all, homemade pumpkin pies— dozens of them. In the Old Country we didn't know of such things, but our neighbors told my mother just how to make them from the pumpkins that grew in our garden and ripened just at this time. The evening meal, which was called *supper*, was pretty much a repetition of the noonday meal.

On the second day of the thrashing, when we had the hang of the job, my mother, my sister and I went out into the field to watch the work. The huge thrashing machine stood close to the stack of wheat bundles, and in the wagon box next to the stack stood two men with pitchforks. They tossed the bundles into the mouth of this hungry giant. There was also a man, or two or three, working on the thrashing machine, seeing to it that the wheels all worked properly. It seemed very involved; so many big and little wheels and black belts going round and round. And the noise!

From a chimney-like cylinder flew into the air a stream of chaff that curved and fell to the ground, forming a big mound. Waist-high to a man was a funnel from which poured the precious golden wheat; two men held a gunny sack under the spout and caught every kernel. Two more men stood ready with another sack to step forward as soon as one sack was filled. It was all so hectic and exciting. I had never seen anything so wonderful. These sacks of grain represented a whole year's work, and were the only currency with which to buy all the necessities for the coming year.

At one point in this operation the men who were supposed to bring up the sack to replace the one that was full looked away for a moment, and as the full sack was removed to be tied and placed in the wagon, the stream of wheat continued to pour out of the spout onto the ground. This was precious gold going to waste, and my mother became very agitated as she watched. She pointed to the stream of grain and called to the men who had neglected their job, *"Shit in der sack!"* which, in Yiddish, means "Pour into the sack."

My mother knew no English, and she had no idea why such an innocent remark should electrify these Americans. The men looked at her in amazement. My father explained to the men what my mother had really said, and they howled with laughter. When my mother learned what her words meant in English she was so mortified that she blushed crimson and couldn't even look at the men. We used to tease her about it, and she saw the humor. But I don't think she ever quite got over it, for although she eventually understood English, she was always very reluctant to speak it.

Two Worlds

How can one bring the close, intimate life of the Russian *shtetl* to the vast open wilderness of the prairie?

It was my mother who called it a wilderness. To my father the life he had chosen was a challenge to his strength, his industry, his ingenuity. He had the physical, emotional, and mental strength to cope with the challenges of this free world. But how was he to cope with his wife's dissatisfaction and bitter disappointment with the life she was now forced to live?

My mother had married a man who had the same background as her own. Their life had been harmonious, compatible, reasonable. But this was not the man she married; this was not the life she could cope with—and yet she had to cope with it. She was a wife and mother, and cope she did. True, she wept, she complained, she blamed, she regretted. She felt trapped, betrayed, lost, frightened. But she coped. She rose early and cooked and baked and washed and scrubbed and sewed. She prayed and observed the fast days and holidays by making special dishes. She never worked in the fields as did many other homesteader's wives, and my father pointed this out whenever she complained of her difficult life—although it was true that, unlike some farmers in the area, he had two sons to help him.

It seems to me, as I look back, that after we came to America my mother still lived more in the Old World than she did in the New. Everything she had known and loved in her youth and young womanhood was there across the sea: her mother; her two handsome brothers; the close-knit community where she knew everyone and lived in close, warm friendship; the quiet, peaceful life; the knowledge that her sons would grow up in the tradition of her people —going to *cheder*, studying the Torah.

In Russia there had always been someone to assume whatever tasks might prove to be a bit too heavy for her delicate upbringing—a servant, or a wet-nurse for her child. When my father left for the New World to make a home for his family, her mother looked after her and her children with love and devotion. She no doubt missed my father, but her life continued to flow without interruption.

In order to make this new life bearable, my mother had to escape into the days of her youth, and so only a part of her was with us. Perhaps her serene and safe life before helped her to cope with the life she found so alien, so physically beyond her strength. She was overwhelmed with it all, and her own unhappiness, it seemed, prevented her from being aware of my dismay at the abrupt change of life.

Stranger

That man dressed in blue overalls with the weather-beaten face was my father. But to me he was, and remained, a stranger. And the days and weeks and months that followed our arrival did nothing to bring this stranger closer to me. I doubt whether my father suspected this. I do know that my whole life had been disrupted.

I remember one gray Sabbath afternoon. It was autumn and the fields were stripped and bare. It was after the harvest. The landscape was one monotonous gray hue, and the wind blew dark clouds across the sun. Winter lurked just beyond the next few weeks. The air was sad and solemn. There was no touch of color or cheer anywhere. I was playing in the yard—my heart heavy—finding no pleasure in anything.

Because it was the Sabbath, the day was given over to study for my father and brothers. For my mother it was a day to remember, even more sharply, the old life, where on the Sabbath she would be surrounded by her dear friends in *shul* and the familiar sights and sounds of the congregation praying. Her homesickness and weariness were too much to bear; the bitter quarreling went on and on.

My father came rushing from the house and ran towards the barn. He came out a few minutes later and hitched the horse to the buggy, all the while storming and raging. He got into the buggy, took up the reins, and with tears streaming down his face said, "Goodbye, goodbye—I am leaving. This is more than human flesh can bear. I have toiled and borne loneliness and hardship to make a life for my wife and children. And what do I get? Tears and recrimination and blame. This is the end. I can take no more. It is beyond enduring. Goodbye, goodbye.''

There was no mistaking his intent. He was leaving and would never return. My father drove off down the road and disappeared beyond the hill.

I continued to play in the yard, but all at once everything changed. The sun seemed to peer through the clouds. The air seemed fragrant and warm. The prairie no longer looked solemn and sad, and there was a silver glow all about. I heaved a great sigh of relief; that quarrelsome man was gone. That stranger who had come into our lives and spoiled everything was gone. My mother would stop weeping; my life would be sweet and serene and safe as it had been before we met this stranger. It would all be peaceful again, with only my mother, my brothers, my sister and me, just as it used to be. I continued to play my games— content and unafraid. The world was beautiful once more.

Then I heard the sound of a horse in the distance. I looked up from my playing; a buggy was approaching. Father was returning. The sky turned gray again; the wind blew cold. My heart turned heavy, and sadness enveloped me. There was not to be the peaceful, happy life I had known. There would be quarreling and strife and unhappiness for us all. My father had not kept his promise to go away and leave us in peace. He had returned. We were all trapped.

The Pollack House

The Pollack house was situated directly west of us, about a quarter of a mile down the road. Halfway between our house and theirs was a deep gully. It was such a narrow ravine that it took only a few moments to reach the top of the other side. But as you walked in it, you were completely hidden and had no view of either house. Perhaps the gully was not as deep as it appeared to me, but I was a little girl and not very tall. At night it was very dark when I reached the bottom, and I would look up and see the stars, nothing else. Our dog Shep would be with me, as he always was if I remained out after dark, so I was never afraid—though it seemed at night as if I were at the bottom of a well.

I remember going for a walk one summer afternoon with my sister Blanche. As we went down into the gully I saw her scratching her head, and I began searching for lice in her hair. Along with our baggage, we immigrants brought lice from the steerage journey from the Old Country. My mother fought a valiant fight with kerosene and a fine comb every Friday, but our heads were seldom completely free of those tenacious pests. On that afternoon, as I was searching through my sister's hair, I looked up and saw Mrs. Pollack at the rim of the incline, coming towards us. I was embarrassed and wondered whether she had seen what I was doing. She made no sign that she had. She was a good, sweet woman who would never say or do the wrong thing. I felt sure that she could cope even with lice. Nothing could ever daunt her—not loneliness or hard work or the newness of America. Her world was here.

I remember one Saturday when Mrs. Pollack came over to visit us. She found my parents engaged in a bitter quarrel. Each was blaming the other for the unhappiness they were both drowning in. Mrs. Pollack sized up the situation, and, without saying anything or trying to stem the flood of bitterness and disappointment which prompted these outbursts, she did the only thing she could do. She rescued my sister and me from having to witness this storm by taking us back to her home for the rest of the day.

Mrs. Pollack was a wise, simple woman, and she had compassion and respect for my parents. She was stocky and sturdy and competent—all the things my mother was not. She had been reared in a less sheltered atmosphere than my mother had, and she was better able to cope with the life of a pioneer woman. I always loved coming to her home. It was a haven, where peace and serenity and order dwelt.

The Pollack house, wooden and unpainted, stood naked against the background of the broad hill rising behind it. There were no trees, no flowers, no bushes; but the yard was swept clean. The windows gleamed with their polished glass, and snow white curtains showed through. It was like a doll's house—so tiny, so neat and cozy. Within was such order that my heart lifted and found the calmness it longed for. There was a cooking range in one corner of the room, but it was not black like ours; it was a thing of beauty, painted silver, and so gleaming and spotless that it glowed. On the other side of the room was a narrow bunk bed with a gay, flowered coverlet. I think the charm of that house was due to its scrubbed simplicity.

The family consisted of husband and wife, four small boys, and the little grandmother who had been brought over from Roumania to live with her daughter in this new land. How they all fit into this tiny house I don't know, but they all seemed to live in complete harmony. Everything was in its place. Everyone did his share. Even the grandmother worked from morning until night so she would not be a burden to her son-in-law. Perhaps, among other things, having her mother there made life easier for Mrs. Pollack. She was not burdened with the guilt my mother felt for having left her own mother behind. Often I heard my mother say, "God is punishing me for deserting my mother."

I still remember that Saturday when our kind neighbor took my sister and me by the hand and led us out of our chaotic home. It was good to leave strife and fury and frustration behind and enter a home filled with serenity. And yet I recall the deep anxiety that clouded the day for me, even as I played at my games and ate the food served on the spotless white cloth at the little kitchen table. I was wondering what was happening to my mother. Was my father hurting her? He had been so angry when we had last seen him. I was afraid of him and his temper and his violent explosions. Was my mother safe? I dreaded going home to the turmoil, yet I was anxious to go back and see if my mother was all right.

I never saw my father strike my mother, and I'm sure he never did. Jewish husbands did not beat their wives; only *muzhiks* did. But I always worried about my mother whenever they quarreled. The new situation I had been plunged into was so strange and foreign. This man I didn't know had disrupted my peaceful world and made my mother unhappy—it was all his fault. And so, whether at home or away from it, I found no pleasure, no peace.

Revelation

I remember one Saturday in spring. Perhaps it was also a holiday. I know it was a good day, because I can visualize sunshine falling upon tender green shoots, a very clear blue sky and light summer dresses. We were having visitors, and there were little girls my own age. We children—my sister and our friends and I—were playing down in the valley below the house where the well was. In spring the melted snow formed a little lake where the mama ducks and their golden, pudgy ducklings swam in a follow-the-leader line. I adored the ducklings; they looked like drops of melted sunshine.

On this sunny afternoon we little girls were having a confidential conversation. One little girl turned to me and asked, "Do your parents quarrel? Mine do."

I was taken aback and shocked by her bold admission. How could one admit such a shameful state of affairs? I evaded the direct question by saying, "I don't know whether my parents quarrel or not. I've never heard them. Maybe they do when I'm not in the house."

This little girl was not a close neighbor. Her family lived several miles away, and we didn't see them very often. Maybe she could be fooled—at least I hoped so. But what puzzled me was her complete acceptance of the fact that her parents argued. Her speaking of this fact seemed to prove it didn't bother her, and that she felt it was nothing to hide or be ashamed of. As for me, my parents' quarreling was such a painful, ugly thing that of course I had to hide it. I couldn't understand why it seemed to affect me in such a different way than it did her.

As I look back, I realize that she had known both her parents from the very beginning of her life. Perhaps this was why she found their strife so normal. I had been transplanted from a peaceful world where my mother and grandmother never raised their voices. This new life of conflict and discord was a situation I was not accustomed to, and it frightened me.

A New Life

School Days

My sister and I started school the spring following our arrival in North Dakota. We would walk across the north field to the home of the Luper family to pick up the Luper sisters, Laura and Minnie. Their farmhouse was a two-story, unpainted frame building. It stood naked and unadorned; there were no trees anywhere. When we arrived at their yard we usually heard one of the girls raising a fuss while her mother combed out her long, curly braids. We would then start across the open fields going easterly, our shadows falling before us.

In the springtime the sun glistened on the new green shoots mixed in with the old hay. As the summer progressed the grass would grow tall and turn steel gray. We would be walking, talking, and laughing, and suddenly there was the little schoolhouse, like a toy building with a toy barn behind it, standing in the vast emptiness of the prairie. We had walked a mile or more.

We would join the children playing in front of the school, and soon the teacher would come to the door and say, "Time to start." We would enter the narrow door, taking one step up to do so. Inside this one-room house were rows of school desks; each class occupied a row. There were small square windows on three sides of the room, and a black pot-bellied stove in the middle. The teacher's desk was at the front of the room just beyond the entrance. There was a clean smell of new raw wood, of chalk and inkwells and varnished desks.

In all, we were perhaps a dozen children, ranging from kindergarten to the eighth grade. There were no older boys. My brothers went to school in the wintertime, as did the other big boys. During the summer they worked in the fields. We little girls stayed at home in the winter because the weather was so severe. I remember going in the sled with my brothers on mild winter days to visit their class. They went to a school that had two rooms and older children.

I remember the bright summer days—playing hide-and-seek at recess time behind the school barn, the smell of the sun-drenched hay, the sound of clicking grass-hoppers, the shrill yells of my classmates. I recall eating hard boiled eggs and home-baked *challah* with sweet butter at lunchtime. It tasted so good! When we walked home in the late afternoon the tall grasses bent before us as the wind swept over them. When we came across a prairie rose, with its five open petals of exquisite pink, and its indescribable perfume, we would hold our breath. Sometimes my sister and I would spend hours roaming the fields and picking the rare blooms; then my mother would make rose jelly to serve with tea when company came.

So many images come to mind when I recall school days on the prairie. I loved it all: the desks in neat little rows; the teacher, who was always dressed so neatly in a starched, white high-collared blouse, dark skirt, and high button shoes. She was always so pleasant and patient— and she smelled so good! I loved being part of this un-troubled, orderly world, where I experienced the camara-derie of my peers, and the excitement of learning. I remember my first book—McGuffy's Reader. I visualize it on my desk opened to a picture of a little chicken exclaim-ing, "The sky is falling, the sky is falling!"

School was wonderful. It was peaceful, orderly, congenial. I was learning a new language and meeting children from different cultures. A whole new world was opening up to me, and I welcomed it.

First Generation American

A little more than a year after we arrived in America, the day after *Yom Kippur*, my baby brother was born. My mother had insisted on fasting in spite of all the cajoling of the other women in the improvised *shul*. There is special dispensation for contingencies such as childbirth, but my mother refused to avail herself of it. She undoubtedly felt the need to involve herself completely, for she was truly devout. Her faith and devotion to the God of Israel was a vital part of her life, and on this Day of Atonement she must have felt a need for divine help. She was facing the awesome ordeal of bringing forth a new life in alien and, for her, hostile surroundings. There was no doctor, no hospital. There was only the crude sod house standing naked and unsheltered on the vast emptiness of the prairie. And there was God, who provided the strength derived from faith.

It was September. Summer had gone completely, and winter was ready to pounce at any time. Father had gone off early that morning to the nearest town, which was about twenty-five miles away. In 1909, with a wagon and a team of horses and a trail that wound over hills and valleys, it was a two-day journey. My father had gone to bring home provisions for the coming winter. He would not return until the following day after dark.

That afternoon my sister and I were playing in the yard when my mother came to the door and called us. She had told us when we went out not to wander from the yard. Now she came and directed us. I was to run to the Luper house just a quarter mile north and tell Mrs. Luper to come at once. My sister was to run and call my brothers, who were working in the field. We did as we were told; then we continued to play in the yard.

A few hours later my brother was born. My mother named him Abraham because he was born in the wilderness. At first he refused to nurse, and my mother was desperate. There were no such things as formulas. I remember my mother asking me to bring the sugar bowl to the bed. She sprinkled sugar on her nipple, trying to coax the infant to suckle, but he only turned his head and cried. I stood there holding the sugar bowl and feeling so bad, both for my mother and my baby brother.

In the Old Country babies were wrapped in a long strip of cloth wound around and around from the shoulders to the feet, keeping the arms close to the sides. The baby resembled a cocoon, and lay rigid and straight like a rod. This is how my little brother was encased.

I remember nothing about the circumcision. No doubt it was all properly arranged by bringing out a *mohel* from the nearest city. A *Brith* is a joyous occasion. There is supposed to be a *minyan* of ten male adults to say the blessing, but I suppose there is a dispensation if it's not possible to have the prescribed number. There is a traditional repast of *airkichlach*, special unsweetened egg cookies, herring, and chick-peas. Other things too. There is the blessing of the wine, and thus the little one is ushered into the bosom of his people.

Somehow Abraham survived the long, bitter winter. When summer came and he was still less than a year old, the long days were dry and hot, as though the wide door of a huge furnace were standing open. There was no shade anywhere. My mother would take white sheets and wring them in cold water. She would hang these wet sheets all about the room in order to cool the air where the baby lay in a pool of perspiration.

The well-being of this new child was a constant source of worry for my mother. In the Old Country, where she had left her youth, her mother, her brothers, her friends, she had also left the little grave of her second born. It had been a little boy who lived a brief two years. That loss had shaken her self-confidence. She never spoke of the child, or of his passing, and it was not until many years later that I learned about it from my sister. Yet always it must have been in her mind, making her even more fearful for the welfare of her New World baby.

Yiddishe Mamma

The term *Yiddishe Mamma* somehow has a derogatory connotation. It implies she is indulgent, permissive, complaining, soft in the head, and, at the very least, a martyr. Undoubtedly such traits may be found in some mothers, Yiddish and otherwise.

But the Jewish mothers on the homesteads of North Dakota, as I recall them, did not fit into this category. Their lives were dedicated to making a civilized home for their families. And added to the burdens of the pioneer woman was the obligation to perpetuate the Jewish tradition.

My mother kept a kosher home, observing every holiday. This was never easy, but here it was even harder than it had been in the Old Country. There was no kosher meat, and hard-working men needed nourishment, so my father learned how to slaughter fowl in the prescribed way. He had a special ritual knife for this purpose and made a special prayer.

I remember seeing my mother make *Chanukah* candles. I don't know what she used to make them, but they were orange, and I used to look at these candles hanging from the rafters in the woodshed. During the eight days of the Festival of Lights she would bring them in and light them as the Jews had done since the days of the Maccabees.

For *Purim* she would fast on the day preceding the lighting of the first candle—*Ta'anit Esther*, or The Fast of Esther, it was called. And while she fasted she baked the traditional *hamantaschen*, cakes filled with poppy seeds and prunes.

I remember my mother arising on Fridays while it was still dark to begin the added tasks of preparing for the Sabbath. Dough was kneaded the night before and lay in a large basin which was nestled in the hollow of a huge feather pillow. The pillow kept the dough warm all night so it would rise. A white tablecloth was placed over the basin, and in the morning the dough would look like an enormous mushroom extending over the rim of the basin. My mother would press her fist into the center of the mound, which would collapse in a wrinkled heap. She would continue to knead it for a few minutes, then replace the white tablecloth and allow it to rise once more. After a few hours the tablecloth would again be lifted into a mound; it was then ready to make the Sabbath loaf, or *challah*. While my mother braided the long ropes of dough into a huge oval, I would have a piece of dough to make a miniature *challah*. At first I could only manipulate three strands, braiding them into something like my own braided hair; but then, as I watched my mother working with four strands of dough, I practiced until I could do it too.

Before baking the loaves, which had risen and been glossed over with beaten egg applied with a goose feather, my mother would take a small piece of dough and throw it into the flame of the kitchen range, reciting a special prayer. It was some relic of the old days of sacrifice—some part of an ancient ritual.

The Knipple

I knew little, if anything, about the value of money. There were no stores where we lived. When my mother ran short of some household item, there was nowhere she could send me to fetch it. There were no candy stores or toy shops.

But I did find coins useful. It was only in the wintertime, when Jack Frost came to visit us. He came early and remained long. When he first made his appearance in October or November, I was enchanted by the artistic designs painted on the windows. First a tracery of ferns and feathers and graceful swirls was etched. Gradually a fine lace curtain was drawn, though I could still see through it. But as the days went by, the lace turned into thick white snow, and I could not wipe it or scrape it away. For weeks and months the outdoors was shut out. It was too cold for me to venture forth, and I was only able to see the outside world through a peephole which I made by pressing a coin on the frosted pane. I depended on this small window—the larger the coin, the better would be my view of the vast world of snow. I believe the largest coin I used must have been a quarter; I don't remember any as large as a silver dollar, for there were no such denominations lying about.

One day I learned that money had another use, equally important, and that the lack of it could create problems and strife. When my father came back from town he always brought my mother a tablet of white lined paper. She wrote regularly to my grandmother and often to her friends in the Old Country. I remember awakening at night to see her writing at the table, the kerosene lamp illuminating the white page. She would dip the pen in the inkwell, writing from right to left, which is the way Yiddish is written. She wrote the return address in English, which she practiced over and over again.

One day the tablet of paper had been used up and it was time to write a letter to my grandmother. My mother and I searched the entire house but we couldn't find a piece of paper that could serve the purpose. There is a saying in Yiddish, *"A guter yid git zich an aitzeh!"* Liberal translation: "A good Jew finds a way!" My mother found a way. She spied a tomato can with a garish red label. Carefully removing the paper, she used the reverse side to write her letter.

After my mother addressed the envelope, she found a new obstacle. She had used up all the stamps and also the money laid aside for that purpose. She asked my father for some money. I don't know whether he too was short of ready cash, but he did raise some objection. What had she done with the money he had given her? My mother was indignant. Was he counting every penny; were we that poor?

I believe it was from that day on that my mother, who had little experience with using money (since all the purchasing was done by my father or through mail order), started the practice of having a *knipple*. Every Jewish woman knows what that is; it's pin money that the husband knows nothing about, to be used only in the most dire emergencies. Many a husband, when in a tight spot financially, has been grateful to his wife for having kept aside some money for the *knipple*.

Food

The chickens stopped laying in late summer. There was no way of getting fresh eggs until the following spring when they would start to lay again. Yet we had edible eggs all through the winter. My mother would take a wooden egg crate and pour coarse salt into it. She would then place each egg carefully in the salt, making sure that none touched. There must be a fair-sized layer of salt separating each egg from another. The box would be placed in the cellar, and because the salt hardened, keeping out the air, the eggs remained unspoiled. My mother showed me how to take a spoon and very carefully scrape away the salt encrusted around each egg until it was free from its cast and could be lifted out. One had to be careful not to get too close to the shell and puncture it. I would dig out a few eggs and my mother would make a tremendous coffeecake, using eggs and butter and sour cream and sugar and cinnamon.

As well as the eggs, our cellar contained wooden barrels of sauerkraut made from cabbages from our garden. There were also dill pickles. But what I liked best were the pickled watermelons. Watermelons were the last things to ripen in the garden. They were round, the size of honeydew melons, and had diagonal stripes of dark and light green. When they were ripe and very pink inside, my mother would put them in large barrels and pickle them whole. I had never tasted anything more delicious.

Also standing in the murky, musty corners of the cellar were sacks of potatoes, onions, and carrots. As the winter stretched endlessly on, our diet held little variety. When the potatoes became soft and began to sprout, that meant it was getting close to spring and planting time.

One day my father came up from the cellar in a rage. He confronted my mother. "The sack of seed potatoes is half empty. Don't you know you must never, never eat up the seed potatoes?"

My mother looked at him questioningly. "What's all the fuss? The potatoes in the first sack were all soft and good-for-nothing. I found the sack in the corner and they were still good, so I cooked them. To me potatoes are potatoes."

She learned, as every farmer's wife learns, that one never eats the best of anything. That goes back into the ground for the next harvest.

Siblings

In the time and place that I'm writing about children did not remain children very long. There was too much work to be done. We each had to do our share, and this meant—except for the Sabbath—working from sunup until sundown. Even on school days I had chores to do before I left for school in the morning and after I got home in the afternoon.

My sister Blanche was too delicate to work out of doors, but I stepped out of my role as mother's helper to see to the milking in the barn and help in the fields at haying time. I also rounded up the cows and drove them to the watering trough. I had my own pony, and I loved riding him through the open fields.

I enjoyed doing "men's work." I often quarreled with my eldest brother Isaac, who was eight years older and felt he could order me around. But things were much smoother between us when we worked side by side in the hay fields. Then I was complimented and treated with respect. Perhaps this is why I so vividly recall those days in the blazing sun. After a long day I would have blisters on my palms and aching muscles, and yet such a feeling of accomplishment, and camaraderie.

It wasn't often that I felt a closeness with my older brothers. Though we lived under the same roof, our worlds were very different. We went to separate schools, and my brothers never helped out in the house—that was "woman's work." On the Sabbath, when there was a cessation of chores, they were busy studying the Torah and discussing Jewish Law. This is how it was for Jewish sons in the Old Country, and this is how my father raised my brothers.

I was quite close to my sister Blanche, though we were very different. She was frail and softspoken, while I was sturdy and rebellious. I remember my mother telling me, "You are like a good cow that gives a full pail of milk and then kicks it over." She would never have said such a thing about Blanche. But, despite our very different natures, we were the best of friends.

I was also close to my little brother Abraham. He was too young to work in the fields or study the Torah, so he was part of my world. I helped raise him, and though I was only seven years old when he was born, I sometimes felt like his mother.

I remember one incident involving Abraham about which I felt very guilty. My father had a little bank book whose miniature size I found very appealing. One day I was playing with the book and put it in the pocket of my dress. Later, Abraham and I went out and tumbled and played in the fields. When we returned to the house I discovered the bank book was missing. When my father asked me about the book I told him that I had given it to Abraham to play with, and that he had lost it. I knew he wouldn't scold Abraham, who was then just two or three years old. Nevertheless, I felt very bad about having shifted the blame onto my innocent little brother.

The Mikvah

It had been the lot of the Jews for many centuries to be dispersed, displaced, uprooted. Yet they had managed to preserve their religion, to perpetuate the ancient teachings from generation to generation, no matter where they landed or in what circumstances. They carried their culture, their religion, their civilization with them. It could all be carried in one hand: the bible, the prayer shawl, the *tefillin*. They also carried with them six hundred and thirteen *mitsvot*, or rules for right living.

My mother carried only three *mitsvot*; that is all that is expected of a Jewish woman. But in reality she could carry only two of the three. In her baggage were the four brass candlesticks which she polished and lit every Friday at sundown from the day she was married, fulfilling the first *mitsvah*. The second *mitsvah*, as she taught me, was to say a blessing over the piece of dough she tossed into the fire when she was baking the Sabbath loaves. The third *mitsvah*, immersion in the ritual bath once every month, she could not carry with her.

Though my father was deeply disappointed that my mother did not share his enthusiasm for this new life, in his own way he tried to do the best he could. After we arrived he started making improvements on the farm. So we wouldn't have to carry water up the hill, he had a well dug just across the yard and topped it with a windmill which would pump the water automatically when the wind blew. The water poured into a huge wooden trough where the livestock would come to drink. Then my father started very seriously to solve the problem of the third *mitsvah*.

He decided to build a *mikvah*, or ritual bathhouse, for my mother.

The bathhouse was a wooden structure built close to the windmill. The floor was made of cement, and there were a couple of steps leading downward to the *mikvah*, which might be compared to a miniature swimming pool. There was a circular enclosure of cement, in the middle of which stood a potbellied stove which heated water for the bath. The windmill would pump water through a pipe which extended through the wall of the bathhouse into this round enclosure. The little coal stove heated this water, which then flowed into a nearby cement bathtub in the bathhouse where we took ordinary baths. It was a big improvement over the wooden washtub on the heated kitchen floor which, until then, had served for baths.

My father used whatever materials were available to make this strange, Old World ritual bathhouse, and he was proud of the results. Everyone who saw it admired it, and was struck by his ingenuity—though I'm sure the blonde Swede who helped my father build it had some tall stories to tell his family and neighbors about the strange customs of the Jews.

Many years later my eldest brother went back to the old homestead to see what was left of it. The house and barn and windmill were gone without a trace. There was no sign that anyone had lived and worked there. None of the dwellings of our three neighbors were there. The prairie was the same—the hills and valleys and gullies. Haystack Butte, the large hill overlooking the stretch of empty landscape, still stood as a sentinel.

My brother searched for some sign—some little token of his first home in this new land. As he walked about on the rise of the hill where our house with its sod roof had stood, he found, in the prairie grass, the cement outline of the old *mikvah*. Imbedded in the earth was a reminder that here Old World Jews had brought with them a bit of their ancient civilization.

Jews and Gentiles

Neighbors

It's difficult to define what the word *neighbor* meant in the days I'm writing about. It was more than just a relationship. *Neighbor* meant friend, family, partner, and much more. Although these people were courageous and resourceful, they were more or less dependent upon each other. This created a bond between them that lasted a lifetime. Since I left the old homestead I have had many neighbors in many places, but those neighbors I knew as a little girl remain alive in my memory as though I had seen them yesterday.

I remember one night in mid-winter. People did not venture out after nightfall unless it was absolutely necessary, but this evening there was a knock at our door. My father went to see who it was. It was our neighbor, Mr. Pollack. He and my father exchanged several words which I didn't hear, and then our neighbor was gone, without even having stepped into our house. My mother looked questioningly at my father, who was hastily putting on his fleece-lined overshoes and sheepskin-lined coat. He said something—just a few words—and then he was out the door.

My mother told us that there had been an accident. The Pollacks had four small boys; the youngest were two-year-old twins. One of the Pollacks' twin boys had been hurt and my father was going to drive the boy and his father to the doctor. The nearest doctor was a long day's journey away—in this case a long night's journey—through drifts of snow over a road barely visible. They could only hope that somehow the horses would find their way, and that they would not be victims of a sudden blizzard.

I could imagine my father holding the reins of the blanketed horses, their breath white in the frosty air that cut like a knife. Mr. Pollack would be sitting in the back of the sleigh under many blankets, holding his frightened son in his arms—and praying. The horses would strain up those huge mountains of snow covering the hills and valleys. It would be long past daybreak when they would finally knock on the doctor's door.

The next morning my mother trudged through the snow to our neighbor's house to help keep vigil until the men and the little boy returned. When I went to sleep that night they were still away. It was well past midnight and I was asleep when my father finally arrived home. He told us what had happened the night before. The little fellow had somehow managed to get ahold of a bottle of ink, and was playing with it when he fell. The bottle broke, and when he fell he cut the bridge of his nose on the broken glass. It was a deep cut, and unless treated by a doctor blood poisoning might result.

We were all relieved when we heard that the little boy would be all right. They had arrived in time, and the doctor had done a good job. The cut was severe, but he cleaned it thoroughly and put in many stitches. By acting promptly, my father and Mr. Pollack had saved the child's life.

Rabbi Hess

Mother took her role as a Jew very seriously, and she was determined that her children would grow up in the tradition of her forebears. What she would never reconcile herself to, and what she feared most, was that her children might grow away from their Jewishness—their *yiddishkeit* —and become coarse, uncultured heathens. In her opposition to such a possibility she was a tigress.

At her insistence our scattered community of immigrant Jews arranged to bring a rabbi from the city. He would teach Hebrew to their children and do the ritual slaughtering, and so prevent the spark of Judaism from dying out.

I remember our first rabbi, Rabbi Brill—a slight, pale, middle-aged man with quiet, unobtrusive ways. He would drive in a buggy from farm to farm, teaching the young children their *aleph-baiz*. I don't think he remained long; the life must have been very alien to him.

Rabbi Brill was replaced by Rabbi Hess, who was a truly remarkable man. When it was our turn to have him as our house guest, my father and he would have long, animated discussions, not only about the fine points of the Talmud, but also of politics and other worldly matters. Rabbi Hess was red-haired, solid, and self-confident, and he met the challenge of his calling. I remember him seeing to it that the one and only Jewish prisoner in the Bismarck jail received *matzah* for Passover.

Many, many years later, when I was visiting my parents after they retired to a resort town on Lake Michigan, my father was reminiscing about the old days. "Of all the people I have ever known," he said, "Rabbi Hess was one of the few I could really communicate with. He was my kind of man."

Keeping House

I had helped my mother since I could remember. I knew how to cook and bake, wash and iron, keep house and clean. Cleaning and rearranging things in the house gave me a kind of satisfaction, and filled a need that I have always had for symmetry, order, and beauty.

I remember a day in early spring. Nearly all the snow had melted; the earth was breathing again, the soft, warm air bringing it back to life. I must have been seven or eight. The yard was a muddy, sodden mess, and it was impossible to keep from tracking some of it into the house. I had scrubbed the floor to the threshold with a brush and brown soap. After I finished scrubbing the floor, I went to the barn to look for a gunnysack to place at the entrance of the house. To my delight I found a brand new sack, un-crumpled and unsoiled, smelling of new fibers and linseed oil. I carried back this beautiful gunnysack, placed it in the space at the foot of the one step, and stood gazing in with pleasure and contentment. I knew that very shortly muddy boots would soil and crumple the clean sack and leave marks upon the scrubbed floor, but for the moment there was order and beauty in my life.

I recall another spring day on the farm. I was no more than eight years old. My mother was away and I was taking care of the house. Rabbi Hess was our house guest. He was staying in the newly built addition to our sod house. It had windows to the east and south, and in the morning the sun poured in and made bright squares of light on the bare wood. I was always happy when I came in every morning to make the beds and tidy up the room. This morning when I entered the new addition, still smelling of fresh lumber, with the sunlight falling in golden squares on the unpainted wooden floor, I found Rabbi Hess folding up his prayer shawl and putting away his phylacteries. He smiled at me approvingly and complimented my sister and me on the way we kept house while our mother was away.

I was so glad to be acknowledged. I was not often told by my parents that I was doing a good job. It was all taken for granted. Everybody worked from the time we awoke until we went to sleep, except on the Sabbath and holidays. Work was simply a fact of everyday life, like eating and sleeping. I remember this one day quite clearly, however, because I felt so proud—so pleased to be appreciated.

The Party

My father looked out over the fields of wheat and flax, wondering how long they could hold out, searching the sky for some sign. He went to bed that night hoping to wake to the sound of rain falling on the parched earth, but woke to clear, cruel sunshine. Later in the day as he and my brothers and I worked in the hay field, stray clouds gathered, passing over the sun and casting swiftly moving shadows. The wind shifted, grew cooler, and began to smell of moisture. In the southeast dark clouds rose above the horizon. They spread along the rim of the sky and advanced higher and higher.

"Come on," said my father. "Let's go home; this looks like the real thing." Excited, we all watched the sky as we drove towards the house. As we unharnessed the horses we heard the rumble of thunder; it was like sweet music to our ears, for each of us knew how much the coming year depended on the rain. It seemed our prayers would be answered after all.

We entered the house just as the wind sprang into action. My mother closed the windows, and we all gathered to look out upon the fields and sky. Finally, a few large raindrops appeared; then there were more. The heavy smell of dust rose up, and before long the rain was beating down in swift strokes. But as we watched in silent thankfullness, white marbles became visible among the raindrops. At first there were just a few, but soon more and more came clattering down, pounding the earth and bouncing as they fell. My mother clutched my father for support. And then, suddenly, it was over. The rain and hail and wind ceased, and, as though nothing had happened, the innocent face of the sun came out again and shone down on the ravaged fields, turning the white carpet into a sparkling sea of diamonds.

The fields of flax, so beautiful and delicate, and which brought such a good price, lay wasted. And the wheat, proud and tawny with their bristling heads full of rich sweetness, lay shattered in their rows like young soldiers cut off in their prime. So much toil and prayer had gone into the planting and waiting for the harvest. Now there would be no harvest. We all stood in silence, looking with sorrowful eyes at my father, who appeared frozen. There was nothing he could do. Not even God could make this right.

The next morning a buggy drove into our yard. Almost spilling over were towheaded youngsters, ranging in age from perhaps three to eight. The father held the reins; he was youthful and as blond and blue-eyed as his children. I had never seen them before. They lived some miles from us, and since the children did not go to my school, and since they were not Jewish, we did not see them socially. My father went up to greet the man, and while they talked we children stared at one another.

My father asked this young man how he had fared the day before, whether his crops had been more fortunate. The young man grinned sardonically and shook his head. No, his crop too had been wiped out. His fields had fared no better than ours. But then he looked at his brood and his face lit up. "But I'll tell you what we did when it was all over," he said. "We got buckets and filled them up with those great big hailstones, and we made a big freezer of ice cream and had a whale of a party."

I stood listening, transfixed. It was as though a new world of light and joy had opened up somewhere in this universe. So that is how Gentiles met disaster—with a grin and a shake of the shoulder, throwing off despair. And with a beautiful party! Oh, if only we could face life like that. It must be wonderful, I thought, to be a Gentile.

The Melting Pot

America has been called "The Melting Pot," as if one who steps upon its shores automatically becomes homogenized. Therein lies a strange contradiction. We humans pride ourselves on our individuality. We treasure our uniqueness, yet we strive to be like our peers in as many ways as possible. This is especially true of children. Immigrant children—particularly, perhaps, Jewish immigrant children—seem to find it necessary, but very difficult to somehow find a balance between two worlds—the life in the home where the language, customs and religion are all so different, and the world of the school, the street, and the homes of their American peers.

In my home I heard three, and sometimes four languages every day. After a time, we children spoke nothing but English among ourselves. My parents continued to speak Yiddish to us, and we answered in Yiddish. Hebrew was reserved for prayer, and this too we heard every day. Russian was also sometimes heard, though it was seldom, and eventually I could no longer understand it. My father used this alien speech when he was especially frustrated with the animals, or when something went wrong with the machinery. By the vehemence of those sounds I knew that he was not mincing words, whatever they were.

One problem language created was the question of what our names should be when we entered school. Our Hebrew names could not be translated into English; they contained gutteral sounds which the American throat cannot utter. My eldest brother was named *Yitschok* in Hebrew. The *ch* has a sound like clearing the throat. His American name became Issac. My second brother, *Yehudeh Laib*, became Dewey in English. My sister *Blumeh*, which means flower, became Blanche.

My own name, in Hebrew, was *Sorah*. The English translation in the Bible was *Sarah*. Unfortunately, another little girl in my kindergarten class, whose family had arrived before we did, had already adopted *Sarah*. Not wishing to have the same name, I decided the next best was *Sophie*. I liked my new American name, but deep down I always felt deprived of something that was rightfully mine.

Separateness

Winter had been with us for some two months or more. The snow lay in huge drifts, and in our school everyone was busy preparing for the Christmas festivities. The two rooms were festooned with Santas and holly and huge cutouts of green fir trees. The crayons and watercolor sets were being depleted in the red and green. Every day we were singing special songs—"Oh Come All Ye Faithful," "Little Town of Bethlehem," and others.

When I say we were all singing, I must hasten to add, not all. My sister and I sat silent. It was as though we had removed ourselves completely, and only our physical forms, devoid of all seeing, hearing, or feeling, occupied our desks. We must have been in the third grade, and at an age when children are very sensitive and want so much to be part of a peer group. No one, neither our parents nor our rabbi, had told us not to sing those carols, but we felt instinctively that this was not for us. The teacher said nothing; she understood. I don't know whether the children noticed or not; most likely they did, but they too said nothing about it.

We were outsiders, just on the fringe of the community. It was not easy, but as the saying goes, *"Es iz shver tzu zayne a yid."* (It is difficult to be a Jew.) There were two other little Jewish girls in our school and they sang along with the others. I disapproved of them at the time, and it made me sad that here was one more separation. But I also understood their need to be accepted, and, besides, their family was not as observant as ours. Although they too were Russian immigrants, they did not observe the Sabbath the way we did.

One day during Christmas vacation I met one of my classmates. She launched into an enthusiastic account of all the lovely presents she had received. Then she wanted to know what I had gotten. I couldn't begin to explain to her that we did not celebrate Christmas, that our equivalent holiday was *Chanukah*, and that we got money with which we could buy whatever we wanted. I searched my mind for some gift I might have received during the year, but I could think of nothing. I remembered a little celluloid duck we had sitting on a shelf in one of our rooms, and I made some vague reference to a cute little duck and other things. Then I said my mother had some chores for me and hurried off.

I remember only one overtly anti-Semitic incident. I was walking somewhere near our school and met a little girl who was not in my class. She picked up a stick and flung it, barely missing me. As she did this she screwed up her face and hissed at me, "Christ killer!" I said nothing. What was there to say? This was not czarist Russia; we were not hiding in the attic. We were in America, and this was just a stupid little girl.

Winter

Snowbound

In my picture books I saw winter scenes. In the center of each stood a house, somehow radiating warmth and well-being, like some contented mother, with broad hips and ample bosom, overlooking her well-ordered life. There was the red barn off to one side, discreetly serving its function like a faithful servant. There was the picket fence, staggering drunkenly over the hills and valleys; and there were trees, skeletal and bare against the sombre sky. Over all lay a white blanket of snow—soft and comforting. These scenes, with variations, appeared on Christmas cards and illustrations of bygone Thanksgiving days.

But the winter scene of my childhood on the North Dakota prairie was an endless sea of white. It stretched in undulating waves, unbroken by houses or trees or shrubbery. Off in the distance the snow-covered land met the skyline, often blending into it, depending on the light. On days when the sky was overcast, there was a feeling of endlessness and suffocation, as though one were swallowed up in some huge void. On days when the sun shone, the brilliance of the whiteness was blinding. There was not a spot of darkness upon which the eye might rest.

Some mornings we would awaken to find that the snowstorm which had raged the night before had piled such drifts against the door that it was impossible to open it. But the livestock had to be fed; the cows had to be milked.

The door from our house led into a lean-to which served as a woodshed. The roof of the lean-to was of flimsy wood, and by poking up through it an opening could be made. My father and brothers would climb out through this opening and shovel a tunnel through the drift, allowing us to emerge from our snow-covered house.

The Blizzard

I suppose all children are fascinated by stories of danger and escape. I remember only one ghost story, that of Ichabod Crane and the headless horseman. I wasn't really frightened enough not to enjoy it. But there were some stories that really chilled me with terror—the stories of the wolf packs on the Russian steppes, standing black and famished, silhouetted against the white winter wasteland, trying to catch the scent of some *troika*. When a pack succeeded in finding a *troika* to follow, I felt the fear of the frantic occupants and the terror of the straining horses trying to outdistance the pursuing wolves.

During the North Dakota winters there were no wolf packs, but we had their equivalent—the white fangs and bloodcurdling howls of the awesome blizzard that lay waiting to pounce without warning. Always there was the dread of being caught outside. We knew the widow, Mrs. Brown, one of our Jewish neighbors. Her husband had lost his life trying to get back from the barn to his house just a few yards away. The whirling snow made him lose his direction, and his body was found the next day only a few feet from the house.

If you saw a blizzard approaching (and you were never sure until it was upon you) and it was necessary to go to the barn to take care of the livestock, the thing to do was to attach a rope to the door of the house and stretch it to the barn. When you got to the barn you took care of the chores as quickly as possible, then you got back to the house by moving your hands along the rope which had been attached to the barn door. It may have been only a few minutes since you left the house, but in those few minutes the whole world could be blotted out.

My eldest brother Isaac told me about a time he and my father narrowly escaped being lost in a blizzard. The railroad had not yet been laid, but the site where the town would be had been established. On that site Mr. Sacks, another Jewish homesteader, had built and opened a general merchandise store. Mr. Sacks, at that time, was a young man with a wife and little children. He had no one to help with the farming, and this store was his way of making a living.

My father and brother had bought several drums of kerosene at the nearest town and were delivering these drums to Mr. Sacks. They started in the early afternoon to make this journey of about three miles. The sun was shining as they drove the sled out of the yard, down the slope of the hill, across the narrow gully at the foot of the hill, and up the other incline; then the road turned slightly to the right and onto some level ground. They continued to follow the outline of the road in the snow, and suddenly the sun disappeared and a few halting snowflakes came down. Then, all at once, the flakes began to come down as though a huge pillow had burst open, and the landscape was swallowed up.

There was not a moment to waste; quickly, they rolled all the drums of kerosene off the sled. My father turned the horses around, but already the road was blotted out. In the ten minutes since they left the farmyard, the whole world had become a white, stinging, whirling universe. Trying desperately to keep his sense of direction, my father urged the horses onward, but in turning around to retrace his steps there could have been some miscalculation.

My brother told me he said to my father, "Pa, I think you should turn a little more to the left." Father got angry and, grating his teeth, shouted, "Don't mix me up!" But perhaps because my brother didn't quite know what a bad spot they were in, he was able to think more clearly, and insisted that they turn a little more to the left. They did so, just a little, and suddenly the horses and sled were in the gully and they knew exactly where they were. This part of the gully was a little deeper than it was where the road traversed it, and so by veering just a little more leftward, the horses finally found the trail. Within a few minutes they were in the yard. They unhitched the horses, and not waiting to unharness them, left them in the barn and made a dash for the house.

Charlie

A few nights ago I heard Marian Anderson give her farewell concert at the Brooklyn Academy of Music. On the following day it snowed quite heavily for New York, and that night I had insomnia. I stood at the window, looking out at the moon shining over the hushed, cleansed city, thinking of the lovely music of the night before. But what I really saw and heard was many miles and many years away.

The moon and stars were in the same position, and I was sitting in a sled beneath mountains of blankets. I was the youngest of the people in the sled, who included my older brothers and their friends, two brothers named Ben and Charlie.

Many years later, Ben, the older of the brothers, became the district attorney. He was able to study law because his two sisters took on the burden of running the farm and raising two younger half sisters. Both brothers depended on their brains, hard work, and the Jewish tradition of learning to make their way in the world. But Charlie, in addition, was gifted with a beautiful voice and was studying to be an opera singer. His voice had opened a door to a whole new world of music and glamour, and it seemed to me that his young face reflected the bright world he was heading towards. He was the most alive person I had ever seen.

It must have been Christmas vacation. Charlie, who was studying voice in Fargo, had come home for the holiday. We were all speeding in the sled through the vast universe of snow and night and stars. There was not a dwelling or a living creature anywhere as far as one could see. It was as if there was no one except us in the whole big world. What a feeling of comradeship, warmth, exhilaration! Then Charlie began to sing. I had never heard such beautiful sounds—taken up by the wind and carried over the endless white surface. Only we and the stars heard it all. He sang in strange languages: German, in which some of the words sounded familiar, French, and Italian. It didn't matter; the stranger the tongue, the more wonderful to imagine the meaning.

Years later, when I had a season ticket to the Chicago Opera and heard many operas, I was reminded by some of the arias of the music I heard that winter night in the middle of a world of snow. Still, nothing on the Chicago stage sounded as magical as Charlie's voice on the most perfect stage in all the world. Later in my life, when the slush and fumes and raucous sounds of a grimy city seemed to be closing me in, I could shut my eyes very tightly and let my mind drift back to that matchless time of sight and sound.

The whole Jewish community took pride in the gift of such a beautiful voice bestowed upon this young man. He was like some rare, precious stone that had been found among the common agates strewn throughout the prairies. Someday he would belong to the world, but now he belonged only to us who knew him as a farmer boy favored by God.

As it happened, the world would never know of Charlie's wonderful gift. One spring day, while he was away studying voice in Fargo, he went rowing along the Red River with his sweetheart and the boat overturned. Charlie drowned, and his beautiful voice was silenced forever. But for me his voice will never be stilled. I can still hear it as clearly as I did on that enchanted winter ride—hovering in the night between the snow and the stars.

Holy Days

Spring and Passover

At last the earth began to stir beneath the mountain of snow that had smothered it for so many endless months. Each morning the sun rose earlier and earlier, shone more brightly, and concluded its arc more slowly. The wind that had been so fierce and uncompromising sang more gently. It held a promise instead of a threat, and seemed to say, "I have whipped and lashed and howled long enough. I am weary of all this blustering. I shall sing a song of hope and peace and resurrection."

The implacable snow had no choice but to yield to this onslaught, and perceptibly began to loose its firm grip on the earth. There finally came a day when here and there a small patch of dark earth appeared in this vast and blinding whiteness. It made our hearts leap with joy and hope. Each day these patches became larger and more numerous until one day all the snow had melted, running into the valleys to form slews. Except for a few places where the snow had been shielded from the sun by some shadowing hill, the earth at last was free.

Father started early one morning, just at sunrise, on his first trip to town since the autumn before. He wouldn't venture to travel so far in the dead of winter, for the treacherous blizzards could pounce without warning. The road was now open and muddy, and the horses trudged all day to arrive by sundown at the town where my father would get supplies for the spring.

Father returned the following evening, and besides the regular provisions, he brought a tremendous wooden crate. It was about as tall as I was then, and when its contents were emptied it served as a playhouse for my sister, my little brother and me. This fabulous crate contained provisions for the Passover. My father had ordered it months before from Chicago, and it had been sent by freight to the railroad station in Wilton. The crate remained standing in our woodshed until the day before the first *Seder* when the entire house had been made ready and cleaned of all *chometz*. Even one bread crumb left in a corner of a room or pantry drawer could contaminate the Passover.

Several days before Passover, when the melting snow had run into the narrow valley at the south side of the hill we lived on, my mother, sister, and I set about getting our home ready for the holiday. Mother whitewashed all the walls and scoured the floors. She made the utensils kosher for Passover with scalding hot water. A stone was first heated in the range until it was red hot. It was then put into a very large pot of boiling water, making the water sizzle and hiss. The utensils were boiled for some time in this water. In addition, every piece of furniture was carried down to the slew and scrubbed and allowed to dry on the bank where the young grass was just beginning to appear. I remember making little paper boats and floating them on this slew, which, to me, was a small lake. After a while the boats would disintegrate and I would fold more pieces of paper into boats and continue sailing them.

The cows loved to go to this slew, and it was one of my chores to drive them home at milking time. I remember how much I dreaded this task, because the damp places were the home of garter snakes that would dart away as I approached. I knew the snakes were harmless, but I just didn't appreciate their lovely colors and quick movements. I used to stand at the edge of this snake-infested bog and weep bitterly, knowing I would have to go in and bring out the cows. With tears streaming down my face, gritting my teeth, and feeling very sorry for myself, I used to round up the cows and drive them into the corral outside the barn.

In recalling Passovers on the homestead, my mind becomes crowded with images of these springtime activities. Like most holy days celebrated among our people, the holiday was intricately intertwined with the season that it marked. Holidays gave punctuation, order, and symmetry to life which was otherwise an endless ribbon of monotony. They provided the exclamation points in a humdrum existence.

Heritage and Tradition

The Jewish immigrants who came to North Dakota as homesteaders were pathfinders. They had embarked on a new life. In the Old Country they had lived, as had their forefathers, in strict obedience to the Law. It was incumbent on every Jewish father to see to it that his children grew up to perpetuate this heritage and tradition.

There must have been a feeling of freedom in the New World, not only from the oppression of anti-Semitism, but also from the tyranny of perpetual diligence in observing so many religious rituals and teachings. These settlers were independent and daring. Perhaps in the Old Country they had chafed at the narrow confines of being good and devout Jews. But here, in a vast new country, they threw off this yoke by virtue of the fact that there was no synagogue, no rabbi, no kosher butcher, and no *cheder* for their children.

Our family never worked on the Sabbath. There was nothing unusual about this in the Old World; any other mode of living was unthinkable. The Sabbath was considered even holier than any of the major holidays. But in the New World not all Jews observed this ancient custom, especially in this harsh world of seasons and crops and toil. Farmers are at the mercy of the elements. If the haying season has too many rainy days, the livestock will not have enough food to take them through the winter. Make hay while the sun shines, and if the sun shines on the Sabbath in haying time, surely God will understand.

There were just so many days for sowing and reaping and harvesting before the frost took over. Most of the Jewish farmers asked God's indulgence and continued working feverishly seven days a week, except in the winter months when the only necessary tasks were caring for the animals, mending harnesses, chopping wood, milking cows, and other similar chores.

But my father asked of God what was coming to him, and in turn gave to his Maker strict obedience to His commands. Somewhere in the Bible it clearly says that on the Sabbath neither you nor your household nor your servants or animals are to labor. Thus it was that on the Sabbath day, in any season, my father and brothers devoted themselves to the study of the Holy Writ. There was no synagogue or *minyan* of ten, but no matter. Each morning the *tefillen* was wound about the arm, and the forehead was adorned with the small black box containing the ancient prayer offered up to God as it had been for centuries. There were the prayers for washing hands, for breaking bread. They did not take too much time or conscious thought. It was part of life, like breathing.

The Holy Days were observed with prayers, special dishes which my mother prepared, and cessation from work. However, for the Day of Atonement, *Yom Kippur*, something special had to be done. Even those Jews who had not spent their Sabbaths in rest and study and contemplation were impelled to stop and remember their training. And so it came about that on the day preceding *Yom Kippur* all the Jewish homesteaders, who were scattered over many miles, gathered their families and started on a journey to a common meeting place in order to observe the holiest day of the year. The farmhouse that could accommodate the most worshippers was the house of the Weinbergs. It was to be our *shul*.

I remember sitting in our wagon surrounded by provisions and bedding. We had started before noon, after several days of preparation. I remember the hills casting longer and longer shadows as we drove westward, and the horses plodding up the hills and galloping down the steep inclines. I remember arriving in the farmyard after dark and coming into a warm, brightly lit kitchen where several women were busy preparing meals.

The scene that night in the improvised synagogue is still with me. It was the large unfinished second floor of a farmhouse. Each woman had lit the ritual candle for her own family in the living room downstairs, and all about on tables and chests stood the flickering candles. As soon as the men had put up their horses and unloaded provisions, they went upstairs, draped themselves in prayer shawls, and commenced to pray. The women took care of the household chores and then joined the worshippers at the other end of the room.

My father officiated and stood facing the Holy Scrolls. I recall the flickering candles and the kerosene lamps lighting up the faces of the praying men. Each one held a prayer book, and their voices rang out in the old, well-known prayers of supplication.

I was a little girl to whom the sound of praying was not new, but that familiar, yet strange, sight made an indelible impression on me. I could not understand the prayers because they were in Hebrew, but somehow I sensed their gravity. I remember dozing and waking as the praying went on unabated far into the night. Our mothers made beds for us on the floor behind the benches where they sat praying, calling up memories of the homeland, and of relatives and friends left behind. They found it sweet to hear the old tunes and to be surrounded by their own people. They prayed with the fervor of those who have been deprived of something they had always taken for granted.

The following day I awoke to find the congregation again praying. They had resumed as soon as their horses were fed and taken care of. There was no cooking that day, and none of the adults or children past the age of thirteen partook of food or drink until after sunset when the first star appeared. I ate a cold drumstick while listening to the services. My mother and some of the other women were praying and weeping, and praying some more. At one point during the services I went down the stairs into the living room and looked at pictures through a kaleidoscope.

I remember going out into the yard and walking sedately with some other little girls. One did not play on *Yom Kippur*. The sunflowers had turned to seed, and their huge centers were like brown pin cushions. We broke off those which were the ripest and ate the sunflower seeds.

They were delicious. The fields had been harvested, and only the stubble remained. Except for the sunflowers, everything was of one hue—the fields, hills, and pastures. Clouds passed over the sun, and the wind blew a coolness that foretold the coming winter. The air seemed solemn, in tune with the Day of Atonement.

The Double Wedding

I remember the Kremenetsky wedding. It lasted all day and all night. The marriages—there were two sisters marrying two brothers—lasted a lifetime. All the marriages of the homesteaders that I recall lasted forever. This doesn't mean that they were all divinely happy. It just means that people stayed married. I don't remember one instance of infidelity or scandal. This is how it was.

The wedding I am writing of was on the Kremenetsky farm, about three miles from our house. It was in the middle of winter. People held weddings in the winter because only then was there time for celebrations. In spring there was planting; in summer, haying and gardening; in autumn, harvesting; and in winter, courting and marriage.

A wedding was rare and of much importance in our scattered community. It was a time of great rejoicing for the whole community when a Jewish daughter was with *mazel*—or good luck—married off to a respectable, God-fearing Jewish young man. This was the hope and prayer of every parent of every Jewish daughter. And here was this family, marrying off the two eldest daughters to two fine, upstanding young men. They were from a small town not far away and were already in business there. It was really something to celebrate, and all the families from miles around came in sleds, bringing with them everyone from the grandmother to the youngest infant.

In this farmhouse they somehow managed to find room for everyone. The babies were put to sleep, and the young children (in which category I belonged) watched the dancing and merrymaking far into the night, then dozed off in corners, on benches, or on the floor.

In the first few years of this settlement, before an ordained rabbi came to our community, my father performed wedding ceremonies. Although he was not a rabbi, he was the most learned of the community and much respected. As there was no other choice, people felt that in the eyes of God and man these couples had entered into the state of holy matrimony with as much solemnity and binding force as if an ordained rabbi had officiated. It must have been so, because these marriages endured.

I don't remember whether my father or a regular rabbi officiated at this particular ceremony, but there was the traditional canopy with the four long poles held up by a man at each corner, the blessing of the wine, and the wine glass crushed under the heel of the groom, symbolizing the destruction of the temple in Jerusalem long, long ago. There were the happy tears of the mother, the heartfelt wishes of *mazel tov*, the kissing, the embracing and the handshaking.

Every table, every sideboard and chest was covered with a spotless white tablecloth and laden with every good thing to eat: herrings and homemade relishes; roasted ducks, geese, and chickens, all of which were raised on the farm; huge *challahs* over which blessings were made before they were cut into yellow slices; and strudel made from dough as thin as the papers with which the farmers rolled their own Durham tobacco-filled cigarettes.

A strudel was a symphony of nuts, raisins and dried fruits, candied orange peel, cinnamon and sugar. To watch a woman making a batch of strudel was to watch a great artist create a fabulous thing out of flour. The dough was thrown over the two closed fists and manipulated and stretched until it was thin and transparent, yet not broken anywhere. These two expert fists continued their magic trickery until the sheet of dough became the size of a large round tablecloth. Then it was placed on the table and painted with a feather dipped in oil. Over this were sprinkled all the wonderful ingredients. It was then rolled up into a long narrow cylinder, cut at intervals, and baked.

There were honey cakes and sponge cakes and coffee cakes. There were schnapps and wine—most of it home-made wine made from sugar and raisins allowed to ferment, strained, and then poured into bottles.

I remember the fiddler standing in the middle of the room, keeping time with his tapping foot. His bow moved over the strings in such quick strokes that the dancers, forming a circle, danced and stamped and whirled until they were panting and exhausted. They danced the *sherr*, something like a square dance; and some of the men did the Russian *kazatsky*, a strenuous dance executed, with much dexterity, by getting down on the haunches and throwing out the legs in rapid piston-like motion. I recall dozing, then awakening to see the early dawn creeping through the windows while the lamps and candles were still lit and the fiddler still fiddling. Two men had on their sheep-skin coats inside-out to represent animals, and were doing a dance circling around one another while the fiddler was playing some Roumanian folk song. This was a dance from a part of Europe I was not acquainted with.

It was all so interesting and exciting. Weddings were wonderful!

A Town is Born

Wing, North Dakota

S ince that day in the late summer of 1908 when my mother, my two brothers, my sister and I stepped off the train in Wilton, North Dakota, I had seen neither town nor train. Except for emergencies, when, God forbid, someone met with an accident or became very sick, there was no need to go to the nearest town. Only my father would take the long two-day journey to bring back groceries and coal. I don't think I missed traveling. The fearsome experience and seasickness on the wild ocean, and the endless, wearisome train ride across an immense country were enough to last me a long time.

However, after we had been living on the homestead for about four years, I began to hear excited talk of an important event that was taking place not far from us. A branch line of the Northern Pacific Railroad was being built about four miles from our homestead.

I remember the day I first heard the train whistle. I was herding the cows and I heard the sound, faint and distant, borne by the breeze across the rolling hills. It was a lost and lonely sound, and yet exciting, because mingled with it was something else. It spoke of people, houses close together on a street, lights, sounds, and towns and cities I had once seen and been part of. There is no more solitary sight than that of a train speeding in the night through an endless prairie, its lighted windows glimmering in the vast darkness. But in that moment there is a glimpse of another life so different that it sets the imagination spinning.

The first building to appear where our little town of Wing sprang up by the railroad track was the railroad depot. The second building was a grain elevator next to the depot where the farmers would bring the grain at harvest time to be shipped by freight train to the flour mills in larger towns. Then emerged the rest of the town, which consisted of similar wooden structures of one and two-story buildings. There was a bank and a post office, two general merchandise stores, a combined restaurant and candy store, and one or two other buildings along the main street leading to the railroad station. In the area around this street were a few residences, a livery stable, a small hotel and a schoolhouse, which was at the furthest end of the town— perhaps three city blocks from the depot. This is how the town finally shaped up after several years. One could see the whole town and every house in it by merely standing still and looking about. And as one looked, the prairies and pastures and hills continued endlessly in every direction.

Civilization

With the prospect of a railroad and a new town, many of the homesteaders in our area began to think of moving and trying to make a life there. My father bought a lot close by the railroad depot and grain elevator. With the help of a carpenter, he put up one of the first buildings in the town—a two-story structure of new lumber. My father had decided to start a business. It was next to impossible to eke out a living on the farm, no matter how hard the entire family worked. Too much depended on the weather. The boys were grown; they could run the farm while my father tended to the store in town.

There was much discussion and also much strife between my parents over the type of business my father chose to engage in. In the Old Country he had dealt in imported cheeses and charcoal. But here there was no demand for such items. Since he knew something about butchering, he decided to open a butcher shop. My mother didn't think this was the proper occupation for a Jew; the meat would not be kosher. My father explained that since the slaughtering would be done by a Gentile, and the meat would be sold to Gentiles, he would not be breaking Jewish law. My mother could not be convinced; but my father, as always, did what he had to do.

My mother's main concern was to see her children reared in the strict tradition of her forebears. Everything in this heathen land seemed to threaten that objective. My father tried as much as was humanly possible to observe the precepts of our religion, but this was America, not the ghetto. He couldn't live the same way he had. He had to provide for his family. He was doing what was necessary. Again, he was bitter and frustrated. It seemed that my mother never approved of anything he did.

One day my father was going into the new town and said I could go with him. I climbed into the wagon and we drove out of our yard, heading east and southeast. After traveling for about an hour and a half along a newly rutted road, we arrived at a flat, alkaline patch of land. We skirted this and came to the railroad track and the depot. We crossed the track, and the road became the main street. On either side were perhaps a half-dozen frame buildings with slanting, pointed roofs and flat fronts. There was no sidewalk then. Later on, after we moved into town, narrow boardwalks on stilts were built along the fronts of these buildings, making wooden sidewalks along the main street, which extended for about two blocks. I remember that when it rained this main street would turn into a muddy pool. We children would take off our shoes, put on our makeshift bathing suits, and have fun wading in the mud.

I also remember that sidewalk in connection with the teacher who taught my grade when we first moved to town. She was a young married woman who later retired to have a family. In those days it was considered immodest, almost indecent, for a pregnant woman to be seen by anyone except her own family, so she would never venture forth in the light of day. I remember hearing her after dark, walking up and down this boardwalk past our store. This is how she got the exercise which even then people knew was essential to the well-being of a pregnant woman.

Our butcher shop was the building closest to the railroad depot. My father and I entered the front door after we tied up the horses. On the floor was strewn fresh sawdust. In one corner stood a square wooden chopping block. But the most important part of the shop was the huge, built-in refrigerator where the sides of beef were hung. The meat was kept fresh by enormous chunks of ice, which my father and brothers cut in the wintertime from a pond near the town. The ice was stored between layers of hay and straw in an icehouse behind the store.

My father offered to relieve his young Irish-American partner, Mr. Kelly, and told him to go upstairs and have his dinner. I followed Mr. Kelly through the back room and up the stairs. We passed through a small empty room and came into a larger one with two windows looking out onto the street. This room contained a small table, two kitchen chairs, a coal-burning range, an iron bedstead, and a crib. Mrs. Kelly was a young, brown-haired woman with a friendly, unclouded face and a clean apron around her small waist. She was moving between the stove and the table, putting down plates of hot food. She then sat down opposite her husband, and while they ate they talked quietly about the day's events.

I was playing with the baby and observing this scene with much approval and amazement. My mother never sat down at the table with us. She would putter back and forth bringing things to the table, and always there was something missing—the salt, or the spoons. I decided that when I got married, I would sit down at the table and eat with my husband, and I would converse with him quietly in this civilized, pleasant fashion. I admired the way Gentiles seemed to get so much out of life. Of course, I didn't stop to consider that in our family there were seven at the table, while here there were only two. I have since realized that, when it came to my parents, I seldom took all the elements into consideration before coming to my critical conclusions.

The Fourth of July

When I hear so-called American patriots expressing their loyalty with such words as "Why don't these foreigners go back where they came from," I am both amused and indignant. They don't understand what patriotism is. It takes foreigners like my father and others of an Old World background to evaluate this country in comparison with the places they came from. They had

experienced persecution and intolerance and injustice, and
they loved this country with a fervor and loyalty that was
not paralleled. It is perhaps because they knew the difference between liberty and tyranny that they were so jealous
of their freedoms, and determined to preserve them.

In our one-room schoolhouse we learned about
patriotism and the American Revolution and George
Washington. "I pledge allegiance to the flag" means very
little to a six or seven-year-old, but the story about chopping down the cherry tree and the little boy who couldn't
tell a lie was very real and immediate to me.

The celebration of the Fourth of July in those days
was always a memorable event, but the one I remember
most vividly was the Fourth of July when our new town
had its coming out party. From the surrounding farms, the
farmers and their families converged as though Paul
Revere himself had sounded the alarm. They came in their
wagons and buggies, dressed in their best—with some
touch of red, white and blue, either in the attire of the
young ladies or in a little flag. As my family and our
neighbors headed towards the town, the excitement
mounted—there were so many wagons and so many people
gathered in one place.

From every storefront an American flag waved, bright
and fresh and clean. In the center of the tiny town had been
erected a platform of the same new lumber as the houses,
still unpainted and not yet weatherbeaten. There was a rail-
ing draped with red, white and blue bunting, and several
rows of boards served as benches. Here the orators would
harangue the crowd, and later in the afternoon the band
would play. It was a time of great excitement and pride and
optimism—though it would not be long before we patriots

would see our sons and brothers going off to fight in the First World War.

August 1914

We had been in this country for about six years. The Old Country was so far away that gradually memories of Russia, for me at least, faded to a faint recollection. I was no longer a little immigrant in foreign clothes, speaking an alien language. Except when we talked with our parents, my sister and brothers and I spoke English. The clothes we had arrived in—the lovely dresses and the velvet coat which had so delighted me—had long been outgrown and discarded. My mother made us gingham and calico dresses on the Singer sewing machine. From Sears and Roebuck in spring and autumn came the eagerly awaited parcels of yard goods, shoes and long stockings, high fleece-lined boots, and long winter underwear. We no longer wore shawls, but instead, sunbonnets in the summer and woolen stocking caps pulled over our ears in the winter. I no longer sang Yiddish and Russian songs. I sang "Pretty Little Red Wing" and "In the Shade of the Old Apple Tree." I learned them from hearing my father sing them in his broken English. I remember being embarrassed by the way my father spoke. I spoke the language as well as any native-born American, and he had come four years before us. I didn't realize then that it's much easier to learn a language as a child than as an adult.

Though my father had started a business in the new town of Wing, we still lived on the farm, and that too had lost its Old World look. An extension to the old sod house had been built from fresh new lumber by a real carpenter. More acres had been cleared; more wheat, oats, and flax had been planted. There was a shiny new windmill whirling in the wind. Our livestock had grown from one cow to several, and there were newborn calves. In place of one horse and a donkey, we now had a team of horses and a pony. We had chickens, ducks, geese, and even turkeys. Our farm was the result of the combined efforts of everyone in our family. We were all busy and involved in this new life. We were American farmers.

But one day something happened that brought us back sharply to the old life. I remember it was a day in late summer—August—in 1914. In our home on that day several European neighbors were assembled. They were talking about Europe. It seemed that the Old World was once more embroiled in its ancient feuds, and what became known as the First World War had begun.

The people in our home that day all spoke Yiddish, but each had a different way of pronouncing the same words. They came from Russia, Poland, Roumania, and Hungary. It made little if any difference to them which side would win. They had come to America because they were despised and persecuted in their native lands. In Europe their children could attend high school only by quota, or by bribing officials. And they could own no land. They had been outcasts.

Here we were in this free land, where our only enemy was the elements, but we could never be detached. Our ties to the Old Country made us anxious and afraid. We were Americans, but we were much more. We were Jews whose roots went back not only to that land across the sea, but thousands of years to the land of Abraham and Moses. We had been dispersed and scattered, but even in this new, strange land we could not forget.

When I watched the sunset that evening it had an ominous quality. My thoughts were with my little grandmother. Was her village in flames? And my mother's two brothers, both of military age—were they off fighting the Czar's war? We knew our family and friends would suffer. From the pharoahs to Haman, from the Spanish Inquisition to the pogroms, we knew about suffering. It was in our past; it was our heritage. We had no way of knowing that twenty-seven years later, even worse tragedy awaited them; Hitler's army would succeed in wiping out almost every Jew in Poland, the home of our relatives who had survived the First World War.

The Peddler

It was only the beginning of December, but it felt as if the winter had been with us for ages and would never end. Our little group of wooden houses stood as if huddled against the onslaught of wind and snow.

One day a stranger drove onto our one and only main street. His low wooden sled, driven by a pair of weary horses, was covered over with heavy canvas. The man wore a straggly unkempt beard, a sheepskin coat, and a heavy cap with flaps covering his ears. He drove his sled up to the livery stable, unhitched his horses, and took care of their needs.

When I came home from school late that afternoon my mother informed me that we were having company for supper and gave me some chores to do. Our guest was the stranger in the sled; he had come to our home selling fish, and my mother had offered him a place to rest for the night.

On the kitchen table sat a galvanized pail of fresh fish. True, it was only herring, the lowliest of fish, and it was not altogether fresh—they were frozen solid—but it was still a most welcome and unexpected treat. We had not seen or tasted fresh fish for as many years as we had lived in North Dakota. Sardines and salmon in cans had but a faint, unrecognizable relationship to the fish caught in the clear streams of the Old Country and prepared every Friday in the traditional way. *Gefilte fish* cannot be compared to any other dish, and it can only be made with fresh fish. Some of our Jewish neighbors had attempted to make something like it with the white breast of chicken, but it tasted nothing like it should have.

I was busy in the kitchen, carefully scooping out the eggs encased in layers of hardened coarse salt. I then began peeling pounds of potatoes, which my mother would grate on the fine side of the grater. My mother was making a huge potato *kugel*, made from fresh potatoes, onions, eggs, a little flour, and baked with plenty of goose fat. It wasn't Friday night, but my mother put a white linen tablecloth over the oilcloth-covered dining table.

As I sat peeling potatoes I remembered the last time a peddler had passed through our town. This one had arrived in a wagon instead of a sled, and the back was filled with many large wooden barrels. The peddler had stopped in front of our store, and my father went outside to greet him. When he returned, he was rolling a big barrel of apples, which he brought into the store, through the kitchen, and into the lean-to at the south side of the house. For the next month, whenever I passed that barrel I would reach in and pull out one of those lovely, delicious apples. In reality they were quite small, and not at all impressive in comparison to the produce we're accustomed to today. But at the time they were a tremendous treat, because no fruit of any kind grew in our whole area—there was just none to be had. So these small, nondescript apples were a rare delicacy.

The kerosene lamps were already lit when our weary guest finally arrived. He had spent the entire day going from house to house—including a few nearby farms— selling his frozen fish. My father greeted the man as all Jews greeted one another. *"Sholom aleichem." "Aleichem sholom"* was the reply. They continued, in Yiddish.

"And from where comes a Jew?" And always a question was answered with a question. "And from where else does a Jew come? From all over the world." "And where does a Jew go?" "He goes wherever he can find a little bit of a living."

My father and the peddler sat talking for a while, and then we had supper. Later, my mother prepared a bed for our guest, using our best feather quilt and the best sheets and pillow. There was a hotel in town, but whenever a Jew came anywhere, anyplace where another Jew abided, he was made welcome. We knew we would never see the man again; he was just passing through. But, as it had been written, we made welcome the stranger within our gate.

Reading and Writing

We had no library in our little town. But we did have a traveling library, which consisted of a narrow wooden box containing about two dozen books. The train would bring these books once a month; then the box would be returned and another one would arrive. I would read every book in that box. The level of the subject matter ranged from kindergarten through high school, but it made no difference to me. I loved to read, and any printed matter, whether it was the *County Farmer* or the English section of the Jewish newspaper, was grist for my mill.

Every spare moment my nose would be buried in some book or magazine. I had very few spare moments, but on Saturday, because it was the Sabbath, I had comparatively little to do. There was no cooking or baking or washing clothes or ironing or sewing. My chores consisted merely of milking the two cows, setting the table for meals, and washing the dishes three times. That left enough time to read two average-sized books.

I remember coming to the end of *The Mill on the Floss*. It was early evening and I was upstairs in the room just at the top of the stairs. It was a bedroom and also a sitting room, with a double bed, a small table, and two kitchen chairs. As the light began to fail, I lit the kerosene lamp and continued to read. I don't recall the characters or the plot—it was so long ago. But I remember weeping as I laid it down and said goodbye to the people whose lives I had shared. I mean to reread that book someday to find out if my fading impressions are correct. I also remember Joseph Conrad and the violence of his people and the even greater violence of storms and seas. There were many books which form a pleasant blur of memories.

I also have some angry recollections of my eldest brother reprimanding me for reading on weekdays. How dare I waste time reading when there was work to be done? There was always work to be done—morning, noon, and night—and it seemed it was always little me who was nominated. My sister was too delicate, so no one bothered her. It was up to me to do everything. And it was always my eldest brother who scolded and ordered and criticized. How I disliked him for being so bossy!

Camille

I used to stand in front of the mirror sucking in my rounded cheeks, trying to make myself look anemic and pale. If I were more like my sister life would be so much more pleasant for me. I would be treated with more consideration; whatever I asked for I would get; my parents would love me more. I was discriminated against because I was so healthy and strong. All the chores fell to me. And I could cry my eyes out for something I wanted, but it would do no good.

When it came to my sister—well, she might have anything she asked for. True, she never seemed to want anything; at least she never asked for anything. I was the one who was always wishing for things: a new dress, a piano, curtains for the windows, a setee in a separate room which would always be neat and dressed up for company. I didn't ask for these things; I knew I would never get them.

Still, if only I were thin and pale and wan. But no matter how hard I tried sucking in my cheeks, I remained sturdy and robust and capable.

There were other reasons why I believed my parents did not love me as much as they did my sister. My mother would point to a faint line on my sister's cheek and tell me that I had scratched her and it had left a mark. I felt very guilty. The fact that it happened when I was a year and a half and my sister was three did not mitigate my feelings of guilt. It wasn't until many years later that I began to see things in a different light. Was it my fault that I was bigger and stronger than my sister when we were still infants? My mother had no right to blame a child of less than two for her own negligence. She should have seen to it that her babies were better supervised. She was shifting the blame onto me.

When my sister and I were both mature women I mentioned to her how I had wished to be more like her in order to get more love and attention. She told me that she had envied me and was sure that I was the favored one, since she gave my parents so much trouble when she was sick. She told me how she resented it when my mother would take the broom from her hand and give her a glass of sweet cream instead. I began to realize that no matter what parents do or don't do, their children will somehow find it's the wrong thing.

My sister must have related to my mother the conversation we had about my trying to look thin, because one summer when I was visiting my parents my mother said to me, "You poor child. So you thought I didn't love you because you were the stronger." She seemed to regret my having come to this conclusion. Perhaps she wished she had sensed it long ago. Now that I have my own children I realize the inevitability of misunderstanding between the generations. It's a shame that we only seem to bridge the gap long after there's anything we can do about it.

Brief Encounter

I remember the first time I fell in love. I remember the hour, the day of the week, the time of year. It was wintertime and it must have been very cold out, because we remained in our classroom during recess. I was in the fifth grade and must have been about ten or eleven years old. I arrived at school that morning, as always, before nine o'clock. It was a morning like any other in the little village of Wing, where the township school had been built just a couple of years before. When I entered the schoolhouse door the teacher was standing at her desk with the large blackboard behind her. She was dressed, as usual, in a crisp white blouse with a Peter Pan collar and a dark woolen skirt of Scotch plaid that reached nearly to the tops of her high button black shoes. Her brown hair was twisted into a bun at the nape of her neck.

"Good morning, Miss Scranton," I said. "Good morning Sophie," she answered. "Let me introduce you to my brother Andrew. He's visiting our class today." As I shifted my gaze away from my teacher I caught my breath. Beside her stood a boy of about my own age and size. I had never beheld anyone so beautiful. He stood straight and relaxed, seemingly unconscious of his elegant clothes—as though he always wore such apparel. He had a pleasant, friendly demeanor, and his face was not weatherbeaten like the boys I knew. His hair was smooth and shiny, and cut evenly around his shapely head. The hair of the boys in my school, when they removed their felt caps with earlaps, was tousled and unruly. This boy wore a dark grey woolen jacket with several matching buttons, and a spotless white cotton shirt with a turned-down collar. His knickers matched the jacket, and he wore black ribbed stockings which ended at the tops of shiny black leather shoes that laced up just above the ankle. The boys I knew wore faded blue overalls tucked into heavy, non-descript boots, all soiled and scuffed, laced up with leather thongs and crisscrossed under metal hooks. Their shirts were of some dark flannel, crushed and wrinkled under the straps of their overalls. In the winter they wore sheep-skin lined coats with huge collars that could be raised up to reach the tops of their caps in the bitter cold. Undoubtedly, this boy I now beheld came from some other world—the world of the city—where one wore such beautiful clothes. He evidently did not work in the fields, or milk cows, or pitch hay for the livestock. I knew nothing of his background, his parents, what church he went to. Of course, they were not Jewish, though it never occurred to me that it should make a difference.

Children's eyes are not clouded with suspicion and distrust. They see purely and clearly the beauty before them. It's later that they take on the burden of prejudice. They learn from their elders who have forgotten what it was to be children, when all children were perceived as brothers and sisters.

The school bell rang at nine o'clock, and we each took our seat. Andrew sat in the first row, closest to the teacher.

I sat several rows behind him, and my eyes were drawn irresistibly to the back of his head. There were perhaps a dozen children in my class, but this day they hardly existed. I only remember the new boy—like a prince who stepped out of a storybook. We had a spelling bee and arithmetic and penmanship. Then it was recess time; but we didn't go out to play in the school yard because of the harsh wind and cold. Instead, we jumped up and raced around the room between the rows of desks. We shouted and laughed, playing as if we were colts in a pasture on a spring day. Andrew joined in as though he had been in our class always. He was one of us. I felt so happy—as if I were one with my classmates, with the universe.

But, suddenly, tragedy struck. My beloved playmate ran head on into a desk, and, with a cry of pain, fell to the floor. I couldn't breathe. I felt his pain as if it were my own. I stood as if rooted, unable to move. He was hurt, and suffering; I couldn't bear it. Often my playmates had been hurt, and I felt sorry for them, but I had never been so devastated. This was a new feeling—more intense than I had ever known.

The teacher came quickly from behind her desk and picked her brother up off the floor. "It's alright," she assured him. "Nothing's broken; you're just a bit bruised." I could breathe again; my beloved was not seriously hurt. My classmates continued to play, more quietly this time. But I was too shaken to participate. When recess was over we resumed our seats. We had history and geography and reading. Then it was four o'clock and time to go home.

I never saw Andrew again. He went home the following day. But I had known true love for the first time. I had felt for another such admiration, such adoration, and such excruciating pain and anguish. Surely these are some of the elements of true love. It didn't matter that I never saw him again. For a few enchanted hours I had beheld perfection.

Beautiful Dreamer

The manager of the grain elevator and his family lived in the house next to ours, though separated by several vacant city lots. I had never been in their home because they were not Jewish, and my family rarely attempted to mingle with any except our own kind. But one day something happened that left an indelible impression on my young mind. I became acquainted with death. The death was not in my own family, but in the family of these neighbors. It came to a little boy just a few years younger than I. The fact that death could come not only to the old had never before occurred to me. It happened so suddenly, in such a strange way, without illness or warning.

The grain elevator held such a fascination for the little boy that he often went with his father to watch him work. One day, while his father was busy elsewhere, the curious child hoisted himself up to peer into the open chute where the grain was poured. Leaning over too far, he lost his balance and fell, and was engulfed and smothered by the grain from which, we are told, comes the staff of life.

For the next few days I watched from our window as the members of the family went in and out of their house. The mother and the girls went to and fro from the dressmaker for fittings; the father and the boys went to the next town to buy new suits. They carried packages from the local stores where they purchased shoes for all the children and hats for the entire family. This flurry of buying was all in preparation for the funeral.

I remember thinking how strange it was that this family, not at all rich, was buying all these new clothes. It was even rumored that they borrowed money to pay for it all. From my window I could observe no weeping, only stoic faces. As the family went about in their calm and quiet way, I wondered why they were doing all this. Was it for their young son who could not see or feel—or was it for themselves? Surely the new clothes could not lighten their hearts or ease their pain. Was it for their neighbors? I figured that for some reason they had to do it this way, but I didn't know why.

One morning my teacher announced that we were all going to attend the funeral at the church, and we were to sing a song we would rehearse for the occasion. A few days later my schoolmates and I were walking along the unpaved streets of our little town to bid farewell to our friend. We were quiet and subdued. This was not like any other outing; there seemed to be a somber silence about it. I didn't know what to expect. I had never been to a funeral, and I had never been in a church where people prayed to an alien god.

As we walked, I began to remember a strange, half-forgotten scene that had lurked in my subconscious for years. I saw images, as in a mirage. It was as though I was recalling a past dream, hazy and blurred, yet I felt certain that it had actually happened.

I saw myself as though I was looking at someone other than myself. I was still in Russia and I must have been about four years old. I was walking with several playmates on an unfamiliar street. Everything about the street was strange; the very air we were breathing seemed alien and hostile. We weren't saying a word to each other until we approached a huge stone building with deep rounded windows that rose above all the other houses. As my eyes traveled upwards, I saw the dreaded cross stretching towards the blue sky. We were clearly in the land of the enemy, and I was frightened.

One of my companions whispered into my ear that I must be sure to spit because we were passing in front of a cloister. If we failed to spit, the evil spirit that dwelled in that building would harm us. I kept my eyes downcast, not daring to look up. My friend, more urgently now, whispered, "Spit!" We both did, simultaneously, and then we began to run as though the evil spirit was actually pursuing us. I remember several little boys streaking past me, with their scull caps on their heads and the prayer fringes around their waists streaming behind them.

We didn't halt until we were once again in the safety of our own little ghetto street. I caught my breath and, heaving a sigh of relief, vowed never again to be enticed into the hostile world of the *goyim*. Here, on this obscure street, where I knew every cobblestone, and where every doorway was the entrance to a friend—this was where I belonged. It was here that I was safe.

I came to as if from a dream, and I found myself walking with my schoolmates. We were at the little church, but it was no fearsome, ominous structure of heavy stone. It was an unpainted wooden house like any other in town, and had no cross to threaten me. The street was not unlike any other. Our little town on the Dakota prairie had no ghetto. My home was next to the home of a Christian. It was good to live in this free land.

We entered the church. The two front rows of benches had been reserved for us. It was as though the occasion was more a ceremony for our benefit than for the elders', for it was one of our little classmates who had departed. The boy's family sat in a group to one side, in front—so quiet and dressed up. It looked as if they were at the wedding of a family member.

This was the only time they could gather to honor their boy. There would be no more birthday parties, no graduations or engagements, and no wedding for him. All these occasions would never be celebrated here in this simple church. That must have been the reason for all those purchases, for the fittings at the dressmaker, for all the new shoes and hats and gloves. Somehow, it made sense to me.

The pastor spoke quiet words of comfort and consolation. Their little boy was safe. The Good Shepherd was watching over him. He would never grow old and weary, but forever live in Paradise. But, in spite of all these encouraging words, we were sad. Very sad.

Then our teacher went to the piano and began to play the opening chords of the haunting song by Stephen Foster that we had rehearsed especially for this moment. We stood up, and in our fresh young voices, we sang:

Beautiful dreamer, wake unto me,
Starlight and dew-drops are waiting for thee;
Sounds of the rude world heard in the day
Lulled by the moonlight have all passed away.

Beautiful dreamer, queen of my song,
List while I woo thee with soft melody,
Gone are the cares of life's busy throng,
Beautiful dreamer, awake unto me
Beautiful dreamer, awake unto me.

The War Years

1917

In 1917 our country was fighting "the war to put an end to all wars and make the world safe for democracy." My eldest brother Isaac had gone off to France along with other young Americans. I remember an enlarged portrait of my brother, dressed in a khaki uniform with a fitted coat and round-brimmed hat. The face was that of a handsome young man with clear eyes, firm mouth, and determined chin. Isaac, who had been just old enough to remember the tyranny of the Old World, felt a staunch devotion to his adopted country. Farmers were exempt from being conscripted, since theirs was such a vital occupation, so he had enlisted.

We were at war. We anxiously read the news. We dreaded the telegrams that would arrive from the War Department. We put gold stars draped in red, white and blue in our windows. When the wounded and maimed came home we hid them in veterans' hospitals, and, except for their families and a few civic-minded volunteers, we forgot about them. To us the war was far away. We didn't hear the boom of the artillery or run for shelter from the bombs. We didn't hear the screams of the dying, smell the stench of the battlefield, or see the trenches and the blood. We saw it, rather, as a sea of poppies in Flanders Field, with white crosses, row upon row. We were saddened and anxious; we wept and shuddered, but life went on as usual.

Here at home we all worked hard and "kept the home fires burning." It was the time of the flu epidemic. It was a time of suffering and sacrifice and hope for a future free from the scourge of war. It was the time of Liberty Bonds and orators on improvised flag-draped grandstands.

We sang many songs in those days. One of the earliest and most popular, which people were singing just before the United States entered the war, was a tentative, pleading song: "I didn't raise my boy to be a soldier, I brought him up to be my pride and joy. Who dares to put a gun upon his shoulder, to kill another mother's darling boy."

We had elected Woodrow Wilson to be our president because of his promise that he would keep us out of the war. Then we entered the war, and people's sentiments changed. Now we were singing, "America, here's my boy....If I had another, he would march beside his brother." We heard, "It's a long way to Tipperary," and Enrico Caruso was singing, "Over there, over there, send the word, send the word over there, that the Yanks are coming, the Yanks are coming...."

In school too we were singing; we had pageants, each child dressed in a costume of one of our allies and singing the national anthem of that country. I had sewn a French peasant costume consisting of a dirndl skirt and a little velvet vest laced with ribbon over a puff-sleeved white blouse. One Friday when our parents came to school we put on a sort of tableau, and I sang in a high soprano, "Ye sons of France, arise to glory." Once I started on a key a bit too high and found it quite difficult to finish, but there we were in the school hall with all the parents present. I went on valiantly, "March on, march on, all hearts resolved on victory or death."

Yes, there was much death, much misery, and a victory that was laying the foundation for the next war. I remember the day we received a telegram from the War Department telling us that my brother had been wounded. We didn't know how badly, and we were anxious and frightened, especially my mother. It turned out that his wound was not severe. After the armistice he came home, bringing a beautiful *crepe de chine* dress from Paris for the girl he was engaged to. They were married, and twenty-three years later both his son and his daughter were in the Second World War. It seems my brother had failed to put an end to all wars and make the world safe for democracy.

My Friend

Besides my sister, I had one chum, Sarah Edelberg. We started kindergarten together on the old homestead, and her family too had moved into town. Her mother had the bakery across the street from our house. We were inseparable. We used to go to the post office together at about ten every morning, an hour or so after the train dropped off the sack of mail. And though the store was just a block away, when either of our mothers sent us to buy something, we would call for one another. We went everywhere together.

My sister and I shared one double bed, and on winter nights our feet were always cold. My friend Sarah had such warm feet that we loved to have her spend the night and sleep between us. It was better than the hot bricks my mother used to wrap in a towel and put at the foot of our bed. I would beg Mrs. Edelberg to let Sarah stay over whenever the weather got to about thirty degrees below zero, which was not unusual. Sarah's mother generally gave her permission, and we would lie in bed, gossiping and giggling far into the night.

Wartime Harvest

The late summer of 1917 was a crucial one in the wheat fields of North Dakota, for there was a man shortage at harvest time. The labor force was greatly depleted because so many men were fighting and dying overseas. So much depended on the few weeks when the wheat must be harvested and thrashed. It was the culmination of a year's labor and prayers, and the income for the entire year hinged on it.

We were living in town that summer. One day the manager of the Boynton ranch, the largest wheat ranch in the county, came into our store. I heard him telling my father how difficult it was to get enough help to bring in the crop. I was interested; I was concerned about the war and wanted to do all I could to help in the war effort. I offered to work on the ranch, and told the man that I believed my friend Sarah would also help. The manager must have been desperate, because he said he would give us a chance and see what we could do.

I was in the seventh grade, and although I weighed less than a hundred pounds, I was accustomed to hard work, both in the house and in the field. I milked two cows, and at haying time I went with my brothers into the hayfields. Holding the reins of the team of horses, I'd sit perched on the hayrake and manipulate the handle that released the hay at the right interval. I had never done wheat shocking, but I was sure my friend Sarah and I could manage. It took two people working as a team to do it.

The next morning a wagon came by to pick us up and take us to our job. When we arrived the field was still moist with dew. As far as the eye could see stretched the shorn fields with row upon endless row of bundles of wheat tied at the center with twine. Shocking involved picking up two bundles, planting them firmly on the ground—leaning one against the other—and then picking up two more and leaning them on the opposite side to form a sort of tent. The purpose was to prevent the heads, which contained the grain, from being spoiled by the rain or dew before the thrashing machine came along.

I can see us now in my mind's eye: two girls dressed in gingham and sunbonnets, like tiny specks in a vast universe. Surrounding us on all sides were stubble fields, golden sheaves, and tiny tents with tawny, bristling heads of wheat pointing to a clear sky that formed a blue dome over the far horizon. There were no dwellings and no trees—only undulating hills and valleys. We felt the sun and the breeze and heard the sounds of insects. We felt at home—as if we belonged there. And what we were doing was so very important. It was for our country, and for the world.

The sun rose higher and sent warmer and warmer rays down upon us. We went on and on—stooping, picking up the bundles, which were taller than we were and weighed about twenty-five pounds. We worked without stopping, except for perhaps half an hour at midday when a wagon came by to bring sandwiches and cold drinks. There was no shade anywhere, except when a fluffy white cloud would pass briefly over the face of the sun. At sundown the wagon came to pick us up and take us to the ranch house. Climbing on, we were hardly aware of our aching muscles as we looked back at the fields we had worked in all day, now filled with a host of little shocks of wheat. It was a good day's work.

The ranch house was a large two-story building, painted white. In the spacious living room stood a piano. After dinner the rancher's wife sat down at this piano and played for us. She was small, round, and feminine, with blond wavy hair and creamy skin. She had obviously never worked out of doors. For that matter, she had not worked much indoors; she had hired help in the kitchen. She was wealthy, and her family had lived here in this country for generations. She was really at home. I remember being fascinated by her arms, which were round and puffy like a baby's, with a line like a rubberband at the wrist. Her hands were white, and looked smooth and delicate as I watched the small, agile fingers on the keyboard. I had never seen anyone quite like her: pink and white, dressed in something pale and fluffy, with an untroubled, child-like face.

We went upstairs where the guest room had been prepared for us. On the coverlet of a double bed lay two silk nightgowns. My friend and I looked at these fragile nightdresses and then at one another. We were grimy from the day's work and the wind and the dust of the field. We had never worn silk. It would take more than an ordinary washing to be worthy of such raiment. On the washstand in the corner were a large basin, a pitcher of warm water, sweet-smelling soap, and fresh towels. We undressed and scrubbed ourselves. Then we put on the nightgowns, slipped into bed between the smooth white sheets, and slept the sleep of the weary.

One day as we were working in a field in a different area of the ranch, we saw the large hill known as Haystack Butte not far away, and realized we were near the homestead where Sarah had lived before her family moved into town. On an impulse, we decided to spend the night in the abandoned house instead of returning to the ranch house when the wagon came to pick us up.

Except for a few days each year when Sarah's father came to plant and harvest a small garden, the house had been deserted for several years. As we entered the yard silence greeted us all about. The barn stood useless and empty.

There was still a glow in the sky to our left as we pushed open the weatherbeaten door and entered the old ramshackle house we had both known so well. Inside, it still held remnants of the past. At the far end of the main room was an iron bedstead with sagging springs and a lumpy mattress. Up against one wall there was a black pot-bellied stove. A small wooden table stood near the dusty window, and on it sat a kerosene lamp with a blackened glass chimney. We found matches, several cans of sardines and tomatoes, a tin chest of Lipton tea, a box of stale soda crackers, and a jar of orange marmalade—all left by Mr. Edelberg when he came to put in the garden. With the aid of a can opener and water from the well we managed to prepare supper, which we ate at the small table.

As dusk deepened we lit the lamp. In the dim light the room seemed even more forlorn. For a while we sat talking of "the old days." Then we blew out the lamp, took off our shoes and stockings, and climbed into bed, covering ourselves with several frayed blankets. The coolness of the night filled the room. It seemed strange to be alone in this house. We weren't frightened—there was nothing to fear. But there was an odd feeling of isolation.

As I lay awake listening to the evening sounds, in my imagination I pictured the night landscape—four houses standing shadowy and ghostlike on the empty prairie. Our house too was now abandoned; and around the bend of the hill was the old Pollack home, where I had found solace and refuge from quarreling and strife. The Pollacks had since moved to Chicago. Now there would be no white curtains in their windows; no spotless kitchen range.

I could also see the Luper house, narrow and two stories tall, with black windows like blind eyes staring into the night. I could see myself running across the field to fetch Mrs. Luper, who served as midwife the day Abraham was born. I could hear little Minnie's cry of "Ouch!" as my sister and I approached their house on our way to school. They had also moved to Chicago.

This house where I now lay listening to the night wind in the rafters had known so much life. Five daughters had primped before mirrors in the dresses their mother had sewn. But the house had also known death. Their second daughter died shortly after they arrived in this country. I saw and heard them all before sleep overtook me. And I knew that I would never return to this place again. That part of my life had already receded, as had my life in the Old Country.

I can't remember just how long we worked on the wheat ranch, but one day, perhaps a week or two later, the manager came into my father's store to pay Sarah and me for the work we had done. He thanked us, and told my father that because we had worked very hard, and accomplished as much as any of the men, he was going to pay us the same wages. Sarah and I looked at each other and smiled. We were very proud.

My Teacher

Miss Kjelland had been with us through the seventh
and eighth grades. She was of Norwegian extraction, and
was small, attractive, and soft-spoken. Besides teaching,
she wrote articles for such magazines as the *Farmers'
Almanac*; and she once told me that she got up two hours
earlier than necessary in order to study law, since she found
that upon arising her mind was the most receptive. She was
also interested in music and subscribed to a periodical
which taught singing by mail. She said I had a good voice
and gave me lessons in singing and voice control. In my
class was a tall Scandinavian girl with a fine alto voice. Miss
Kjelland taught us duets and spent a great deal of time
with us.

The week before graduation my teacher was to marry
the bank teller, who would be going off to war. She had
a great deal to do to prepare for the wedding, so organiz-
ing our graduation became secondary. She turned to me
for help. We decided that I would write a play in which the
whole graduating class, which consisted of about a dozen
girls and one boy, would take part. I remember that one
boy, because he threw a monkey wrench into the whole
thing. I wrote a very simple play in two acts. In the first
part each graduate would speak of what the future might
hold for them. The second act was supposed to take place
several years later, and divulged what actually happened
to the class. I hadn't worked it out completely, but when
rehearsal started and I gave out the parts, this one young
man with red hair and an independent spirit said flatly that
no girl was going to tell him what to do. That was the end
of that part of the program. Had we really been able to look

into the future, we would have been more cooperative—even that rebellious boy who refused to take orders from a girl. Several years later we learned that the soldier our teacher married did return, but only to die in the flu epidemic. Afterwards, she became a missionary and went to the Far East.

Miss Kjelland was a wonderful woman, and she shaped my life beyond the short while that I knew her. In those days going to high school was not mandatory. Since there was no high school in our town, few grammar school graduates went on much further scholastically. An eighth grade education was considered pretty advanced for our small rural community, which consisted of farmers and a handful of shopkeepers. Most teachers were graduates from the eighth grade who had a year or two of normal school. Miss Kjelland must have been a high school graduate, and it was because of her that I was able to go to high school.

It was June, just a couple of days before I'd graduate from grammar school, and the hot, dry prairie had already turned to fields of hay. I was upstairs, just above the butcher shop. The windows were wide open, and I was busying myself with the endless chores of sweeping, dusting, and making beds, when I heard my teacher speaking to my father. They were outside the shop on the wooden sidewalk. I came close to the window and listened, for the voices drifted up clearly and distinctly. My teacher was saying, "Your daughters are the brightest pupils in the school. It would be a pity if they did not continue their education in high school. You should, in all fairness, make an effort to send them on further in their studies." She spoke earnestly. My father listened without interrupting. Then he said, "Thank you. We shall see."

I was so excited I could barely breathe. I made no sound, and I never told my father that I had overheard this conversation. I knew that he would consider my teacher's advice. He held all teachers in high regard, and this one in particular. She was bright and pretty, and so direct. I knew that my father, raised in the tradition of the Old Country, did not consider girls in the same category as boys when it came to education. Learning was largely confined to the male population. In fact, it was the duty of every father to see to it that his sons were taught as much of the Torah and Talmud as they could absorb. I knew that my asking my father to let us go to high school would do no good. The nearest one was far away, and would be very expensive. But now that my teacher spoke on our behalf, I felt that my sister and I had a chance.

As it happened, when September came, my sister and I boarded a train headed for Minneapolis. There we attended school and lived with a family who had been our neighbors before moving to the city.

Graduation Day

In our tiny community elementary school graduation was an event of great importance. As far as I knew it would be my only graduation, and it did turn out to be a memorable evening.

On the morning train a box of white carnations had arrived, one for each of the graduates. This may seem of little importance to people who live in climates where flowers are available any time, but the soil of our part of the country could nurture neither trees nor flowers in abundance. So the small white carnations arriving from the nearest nursery miles away marked an important event.

In the early afternoon of that day the County Superintendent of Schools also arrived. He lived in the capital of the state and had come especially to present the diplomas and give the commencement address. My sister was to give the valedictory address, and I would sing a lullaby.

The Superintendent, Mr. Parson, brought with him his own daughter, who was about my age. The little girl was named Dorothy, and she and I became friends at once. Since she could play the piano, my teacher suggested that she accompany me when I sang the lullaby. She came back with me to my house to rehearse. It was a very simple song, and we spent perhaps thirty minutes going over it. Later, as we walked back to the schoolhouse, she told me of the plays and concerts and movies she attended in the fabulous city where she lived. I was envious of her sophistication, and excited when she suggested I visit her during the summer vacation. I figured it must have been her father's idea to invite me, but I didn't mind. I welcomed the opportunity to visit Bismarck and see how people lived in a big American city.

Soon after we arrived back at school the assembly began. I remember the speech this real honest-to-goodness Yankee, the Superintendent, made. He spoke warmly and simply of the great achievements of these young people, especially the few who had been born in the Old Country. This was the category in which my sister and I belonged; perhaps that's why I remember his speech after all these many years. He pointed out how these foreign-born children had excelled to the point where one of them was the Valedictorian. He spoke of the parents who had made a home in a new, strange land and had adapted so well, and of the sons and brothers who had gone off to fight for their adopted land. He made us feel very proud and important.

The program progressed very well. My sister gave the valedictory speech in her clear, soft voice, without a trace of a foreign accent. Later, I sang my lullaby accompanied on the piano by my new friend Dorothy.

When the commencement exercises were over I walked home with my sister and parents, holding my diploma rolled up in a slender white scroll. It was a clear June night. The stars were bright and close, and the few houses showed dim lights. I had walked through that little prairie town hundreds of times, day and night, yet this one time stands out sharply in my mind. I can still feel the fresh, cool air and see the houses silhouetted against the luminous sky. I was so very aware of myself that night. I was precious to myself—unique and wonderful. There was no one just like me. Somehow I felt specially endowed; just a little more gifted, more aware, more everything.

But I also remember thinking that I would be willing—painful though it might be—to give up part of my precious uniqueness for something which I did not have. I would have exchanged my own enchanted being for a duller, less gifted one if I could have had a happier, more harmonious and peaceful life with my family. I wanted a home free from strife and disorder. Yes, I remember that night. I was willing to make a bargain with the fates that had given me some rare quality, but short-changed me on something else.

Remembering

Vanished Past

Of all the faculties, I believe memory to be the most valuable. Memory is the essence of all experience: all that we have seen, felt, hoped, dreamed. It is as though we open a tiny bottle of perfume and sniff the fragrance. The myriad of blooms that went into its contents are long since withered, but in the whiff as we remove the cork, lies the garden where once the flowers grew.

Our eyes may be dimmed, our steps halting, our limbs weary and creaking. The reflection in the mirror is some stranger we hardly know. But when we open the door to the long corridor that leads back to our youth, it's as though we have never been away. Our parents, brothers, sisters, the children we went to school with, they are all there, going about their lives as usual. And you are there, big as life, with clear eyes and swift bounding steps. The mirror must be lying.

There's no way to refresh my memory. The little town that was once my home is no longer the same. The houses where we and our neighbors lived are not there anymore. The rutted, muddy road where the wagons drove into town is gone. Concrete, like asphalt lava, has covered the spaces. Parking lots instead of hitching posts, automobiles instead of buggies, trucks instead of wagons.

The houses that I remember, with their narrow windows, where the kerosene lights flickered dimly at night, are all gone now. Electric lights now brightly illuminate the streets, blotting out the starlight that once lit the night.

There is only one way for me to go back, to open the door upon the vanished past—by recalling the bygone days. Perhaps in the cemetery I might find some headstone with an old, familiar name, but it's not likely. All the families I knew, like my own, have long since moved away, and their remains lie buried elsewhere. But since there is no way to prove their disappearance, for me the little town and its inhabitants remain ever the same—like photographs in an old album.

Besides the railroad track, the depot would still be there, though perhaps not on the same spot, and most certainly not the same structure. It would be replaced by something modern like the rest of the town.

There is one other thing that would remind me of the old days. That is the grain elevator, towering several stories above the depot—a landmark and symbol of the wheat fields. After the harvest, the farmers would bring the golden wheat to this granery to be stored and later shipped on the train to the flour mills in the twin cities of Minneapolis and St. Paul. The grain would now be brought in trucks along concrete highways, and not, as I remember, in wagons drawn by a team of horses along narrow roads barely visible in the prairie grass.

The Gingham Dress

From Sears and Roebuck came several yards of plaid gingham and two pairs of black patent leather slippers for my sister and me. With the gingham my mother sewed two identical dresses, which we wore for the first time at the Passover Seder and afterwards to school. I had one other dress to change into, but it was old and faded and I don't remember it well. The gingham dress I do remember. The colors were bright blue, darker blue, yellow and white. It was a Scotch plaid, with well-defined blocks of color that stood out brightly when the dress was new. But after much exposure to the sunlight and many washings, the colors faded and lost their vivid hues.

When we moved into town I wore this dress every day, though it had been laundered so many times it no longer looked new. One day I saw my reflection in a window upstairs which, for some reason, served as a mirror. Somehow, reflected in this glass, the colors looked as deep and vivid as they had when the material was new. I kept looking at this reflection, then down at the dress. Each time I looked down I was disappointed by the faded hues. Then I would look at the glass again and wish with all my might that somehow those colors could be transferred to the dress itself. I knew it couldn't be done so I finally walked away, trying to retain the window picture in my mind.

I still maintain deliberate illusions; the only difference is that now it's my memory that serves as the false mirror. For a while I was unhappy about growing old. I asked myself why. My reason told me that it's inevitable. It's the price we pay for living. But then I noticed that I didn't think about it much except when I glanced into a mirror. Looking at my reflection, I would be shocked at what I saw. But when I didn't look I wasn't aware of being old. I felt no different from the way I felt twenty or thirty years ago.

In my mind's eye I see myself as a slim young woman with an unlined face and brown hair unstreaked with gray. Why subject myself to the pain of reality by looking into the mirror? Fooling myself? Perhaps. But since I don't go about wearing a mask or any other disguise, I'm not really a fraud. I am simply trying to ease the path on my downhill journey.

Chokecherries on the Hill

Northwest of our house, about half a mile away, the Edelberg house stood on a level bit of ground at the foot of a long, low hill. Beyond this hill began a further ascent for perhaps a quarter of a mile. This was the base of the highest hill in the whole area. It was known as Haystack Butte because it was shaped like a haystack.

In the spring, in the summer, and in the autumn, we children would climb the hill. It was steep and quite difficult to reach the top. By the time we reached the base we had already climbed some lesser hills. Then we'd look up and see the final ascent looming before us, and know we were really in for some huffing and puffing.

In the springtime we would be on the lookout for birds' nests. The sight of a bird suddenly rising from the grass in front of us meant that we had stumbled onto her nesting place. We would walk very carefully, peering down, parting the grass, and soon we would find what we were looking for—a small, round basket of prairie hay, the size of a baby's palm. Nestled within would be three tiny eggs, the color of blue sky after the rain when the sun first reappears. We would stand motionless, then kneel down and gaze, enraptured, at the beauty and magic of this miracle. We never touched the nest or the eggs. Merely gazing upon their miniature, fragile beauty was enough for us. We didn't linger long, though we would have liked to. Somehow we sensed the anxiety of the mother, who was waiting for us to move off so she might return to her precious and dedicated role of creativity.

As we walked we were aware of so much life hidden from us. There were gopher holes and badger holes and rabbit holes. There were ant hills, and there were thistles and pussy willows. As we continued to climb there were large rocks protruding from the side of the hill. We would follow a faintly outlined path, one which seemed less steep, and as we went up the wind would blow stronger. We'd finally reach the summit, and here the wind was king. Walking about on the summit we could look out for miles and miles in every direction. There were no towns or trees or rivers or lakes. Except for our house and the houses of our few scattered neighbors, there was nothing for miles— only rolling hills and prairie grass.

In the autumn we would look for chokecherries on the side of Haystack Butte. These were little black cherries the size of large peas, in the center of which were small stones like miniature cherry pits. The cherries had a tart, sweet taste, and they grew on bushes close to the ground, with but a few cherries on each. The bushes grew in very few places; after an hour's search we might find barely a cupful, were we to put them in a cup. We would eat them as we found them. They were a wonderful treat, for this was a barren land without fruit or berries, either wild or cultivated.

There was one more treat in autumn. That was the tiny red apple, the size of a small grape, which was the pod of the wild rose. It had a pleasant taste, and was also mighty rare.

I have lived in many places since that first home in the New World, and I have no desire to revisit any of them. But I do sometimes think of going back to the old homestead. I know that there is not even one stick or stone to mark the place where our house or those of our three neighbors stood. Though still, I should not go there in vain, for the hills and valleys, and, most of all, Haystack Butte would still be there, giving me a sense of timelessness, of order and continuity. I should like to walk the now perhaps erased trail up the side of the butte. The ghost of that little girl who was would take my hand and somehow, together, we would find the trail. I would feel the same sun and wind upon my face, breathe the same prairie-scented air, and feel my spirit expand and soar in the free, open, unspoiled land of my youth. I feel that I should be reborn again in that moment, and the gap between me and my little grand-daughter, who is now just the age I was, would disappear, and the chain of continuity would become a tangible thing.

But a cold wind blows upon my spirit as I remember the atom bomb. Man's ingenuity has contrived a way to defeat the universal order. I want so desperately to know that only the elements will continue to buffet my indestructible hill—the harsh elements, so gentle and kind in comparison. I send up a silent prayer that, somehow, sanity may yet win out, and all our beginning's never come to an end.

Please God, please man, let the children continue to pick chokecherries on the hill.

Years Later

Only Human

It hasn't been easy to write this chronicle of my childhood. I've shed many tears in the process. I could not have written these things before; it was necessary to let the years create a buffer zone so that I might be able to stand back and put it all in the proper perspective.

When I was a child I could not see my parents as people. I could see only how their behavior affected me. The fact that they too had needs never occured to me. They were adults; they were all powerful. It was *their* fault that our lives were fraught with strife. My father should not have been so angry and demanding. My mother should have been more organized, a better housekeeper, less complaining, and more aware of my needs. It was all their fault. They just didn't care how miserable I was. Everything, all my unhappiness, was all because of them. I often wished I could have had some other people as my parents. I would gladly have exchanged them for some pleasant, easy going, calm couple. I saw nothing but faults.

I have remembered it all—weighed the bad and the good, the weak and the strong—and I can now tell myself, honestly, that I would not change my parents for any other. They had integrity, honesty, fidelity, character, compassion. Now that I can see them from a more mature perspective, I realize that their strengths outnumbered their weaknesses. I wanted them to be perfect, but they were only human.

The Black Years

I had always believed that the other homesteaders had fewer problems than we had—that there was more harmony and contentment in their lives than in ours. However, when I look back on the entire scene, including all the homesteaders that I was acquainted with, I realize that we were not so different. All of our neighbors came to this country with the same objectives as my father, and they too were eventually forced to abandon the land. The best land had been taken up by the large wheat ranches, which were owned by people of means who had been there for generations. The land which the government gave to the homesteaders was the poorest, most hilly, most rock-strewn, and the most difficult to clear and cultivate. The elements, too, conspired to defeat the homesteaders.

Many years after we left the farm I was reunited with some of our neighbors from the Dakota days, and I was surprised to learn that their experience was no different from ours. In this family there had been six adults and two young children, all working and striving to make a life on the stubborn land. Their family, like ours, had been forced to leave their homestead after several years of frustration and superhuman struggle.

On the occasion of this meeting we were all descending the other side of the hill at varying rates of speed, and five of the adults were with their Maker. Only three of the younger neighbors were there recalling the past. Lilly was several years older than I, and she had worked as hard as any man. At one point in the evening she brought out an old family photograph which had been taken on the homestead when she was still a little girl. Holding the picture, she made one simple remark which made a lasting impression on me. She said, as she looked at the photograph, "I call those the black years."

So, it was not just the incompatibility of my parents that created problems. And had they really failed? They had each held up their end. Yes, they had complained and stormed and blamed one another, but they had continued to work side by side, and had done the very best they could. Considering the tremendous hardships and obstacles, they managed as well as could be expected. We had all been in it together, and, somehow, we had all survived.

Strangers No Longer

We learn to love too late. Only in retrospect can we evaluate the worth of a human being. While we deal with those closest to us, we're blinded by the annoyances and irritations that must enter every relationship. Our very involvement hinders our appreciation. We can stand back and be amused by the foibles of a stranger, but from our own we expect perfection.

I feel sure that my own children are no less critical of me than I was of my parents. I tell myself that this is as it should be. But I also know that the time will come, sooner or later, when they'll see me as just another human being, with the shortcomings and virtues of all human beings. When that time comes, I don't think they'll judge me too harshly. Perhaps they'll judge me less harshly than I judge myself.

When I finally saw my parents as two human beings who did the very best they could, I blamed neither one nor the other for anything. But this took a long time. It always takes too long. My mother used to say, "One lives a hundred years and dies a fool."

I remember visiting my parents' farm near Lake Michigan one summer when our son was still in grammar school. My parents had a house and a few acres off the main road, just a few minutes walk from a vast stretch of sandy beach. Even at the height of the resort season the beach would be sparsely sprinkled with bathers. One could have the lake and the beach to oneself for miles, and it gave me a feeling of solitude which I could never get in the city, and which I find very necessary sometimes.

I recall sitting on my parents' lawn one evening when my father came up and put his hand on my shoulder. "It's good to have you here, daughter," he said. "This place belongs to you and the others. It's as much yours as mine." I realized, perhaps for the first time, how much the years of disappointment had covered over the warmth and gentleness that lay buried within my father. I also realized that he too had been cheated of my love and understanding. After all these years, we were strangers no longer.

Israel

In 1953 my parents emigrated to Israel. They were carried on the wings of an eagle, as had been prophesied in the Bible. It was the first time they had ever been on a plane. My mother wrote to me, "Old Jews come here to die. Your father and I came here to do what we can to help build the new country. If only we were younger." They were both nearing eighty.

My father planted a garden in the yard of his little house near the Mediterranean. The first year the corn did not thrive; it had been watered too much. But he soon learned the proper way to irrigate the land. When the next planting was harvested, there was enough to share with all the neighbors.

Life in the new country was not easy for my mother. She wrote asking that I send her a mop stick, for it was too difficult at her age to wash floors on her hands and knees. In Israel there were no factories manufacturing such conveniences as mop sticks. My father, on the other hand, would write, "Daughter, don't send us packages, send us guns. We are surrounded by the enemy." For him, it was happening all over again. This time it was the Arabs instead of the Russian cossacks. And there was my father, as ever, still anxious to defend his people.

My mother would write, in Yiddish, "Dear daughter, guard your health." My father would write, "Dear children, live life to its fullest." These two directives from my parents, perhaps more than anything else, exemplified where they placed the most importance.

When my mother's coat was stolen she explained to me that some of these people had been so brutalized in Hitler's concentration camps that they had lost their sense of ethics. And when the packages I sent her were rifled at the post office, she would tell me that the girls who worked there got such little pay, that if they were tempted by a pretty scarf which I had sent, she could not really blame them. She was understanding and indulgent—the country was so poor. These were her poor people; she felt for them, for their past persecutions and torment. She would not sit in judgment. She remained as she had always been— dedicated to her people and to her children.

Even after she had taken to her bed, my mother would not let the four walls close her in. She would write of the neighbor's children, dressed in their bright raincoats, standing at the entrance of her room, not venturing in. The children had come to get vegetables from Father's garden. "Children are a little afraid of old people. They prefer to remain at a distance," she explained. She had a great deal of insight, and could identify even with children.

When she knew her end was near she wrote, "We have lived beyond our allotted three score and ten. God has spared us. When our time comes, do not grieve." Now she is at rest in the land of her forefathers, and her daughter must grieve.

In spite of the separateness of my parents' worlds, living together for all those years somehow welded them together. Once again my father was waiting for a reunion with my mother.

After she had been laid to rest in the cemetery of Naharia, my eldest brother visited my father in Israel. On his way back to his home in Chicago he visited me and gave me a report. "Father kept saying Mother's name aloud," he told me. My brother said to him, "Why do you say Mother's name all the time?" Father would be quiet for a while and then do it again. My brother would remind him of it. Finally my father said to him, "Son, I appreciate you coming all the way from Chicago to visit me, but I'll be glad when you go back. Then I can call your mother's name to my heart's content without being told to stop." My brother shook his head in bewilderment as he told this to me. But it's not hard to understand.

My neighbor took a trip to Israel and visited my father, and she too brought back a report of how he lived. She said, "He has a nice little house, and one could do much to fix it up. But all he has is a small table, two chairs, a narrow bed, one cup, and one plate." I knew my father. That was all he wanted. When my mother died he told the neighbors to come in and take whatever they wanted, and they did.

When my father was in his late eighties some of my cousins went to visit him and were amazed at his clarity of mind. He would start relating an episode, and then branch off into several avenues of thought; then he would stop and become concerned lest he would forget—but always he came back to the original mainstream of the discourse. He was always on guard, looking for signs of senility; but always he was gratified to find that it had not yet reached him. When this was reported to me, I found it reassuring that my father still held the reins of his thoughts with as much strength as he had held the reins of his horses traveling down the steep hills when I was a little girl.

My brother visited my father in Israel often. Although his faculties were always as sharp as ever, each time my father complained of feeling weak. He would say, perhaps more to himself than anyone else, "We pray for long life, so why do we complain to God for growing old?" He had never known what it was to be weary, but now he was weary of life. He would say, "It is enough already." But he knew it was not up to him.

Despite my father's bodily weaknesses, he insisted on remaining independent. On several occasions my brother tried to persuade him to move to a nursing home, but each time my father refused. Once he compromised and allowed my brother to hire someone to help him take care of the house; but it wasn't long before my father got rid of the woman. He gave two reasons. He said the woman was "stupid," and he couldn't stand stupid people; and he said she was cold, and pushed him away when he attempted to "snuggle up." All he wanted was a little comfort. My father was a warm, affectionate man, and he missed the closeness of a woman after my mother died. My brother couldn't understand why an old man would still need the nearness of a woman. I think he was shocked at the thought. But I understand. Getting old does not quell the need for human warmth and contact.

On my brother's last visit to Israel my father finally consented to move to a nursing home, and my brother felt he would no longer have to worry. All the arrangements were made: the house had been rented and everything was packed. My father was to leave the following morning.

It was the Sabbath, and my father and brother had both returned from *shul* after the evening prayer. After the *Havdolah*, the blessing for the coming week, they partook of the evening meal. I remember in the old days how Father would usher in the new week at the end of the Sabbath when the first star appeared. He would fill a wineglass to the very top with milk, say a prayer, and drink it. He explained that the reason the glass had to be filled to the brim was so the week would be full of all goodness.

After Father had blessed the coming week he went to sit in the garden and listen to the evening sounds. Soon he retired for the night. A few hours later he called to my brother, complaining of pain. My brother went to call the doctor. While they waited, my father said, "I didn't know it was so difficult to die." He had never known physical pain, and now he was experiencing that too. Yes, his life was now as full and complete as the ritual *Havdolah*.

He did not suffer long. When the ambulance arrived my father no longer had need of it. He was home at last; and he and mother were reunited once more—this time in *der emeseh velt*, the true world.

Harry Turnoy in Israel, 1959

Glossary

Aleph baiz: The Hebrew and Yiddish alphabet.

Brith: Ritual circumcision on the eighth day after birth.

Challah: Braided white bread prepared for the Sabbath.

Chanukah: Holiday commemorating the victory of the Jewish resistance under Judah Maccabee over Syrian forces which sought to enslave Israel.

Cheder: Elementary Hebrew school.

Chometz: Food prohibited on Passover.

Goyim: Gentiles.

Hasidim: An orthodox Jewish religious sect.

Havdolah: Ritual marking the conclusion of the Sabbath.

Kashruth: Jewish dietary code.

Kugel: Pudding.

Kosher: Conforming to Jewish dietary law.

Matzah: Unleavened bread eaten on Passover.

Mezuzah: A small inscribed scroll contained in a protective case placed at the right door post.

Minyan: Quota of ten Jewish males required for religious services.

Mohel: One authorized to perform ritual circumcision.

Muzhik: A peasant in czarist Russia.

Passover: Holiday commemorating Jewish liberation from slavery in Egypt.

Peyes: Earlocks worn by orthodox Jews in observance of the commandment, "You shall not clip your hair at the temples or mar the edges of your beard."

Pogrom: An organized massacre of the Jews.

Purim: Holiday commemorating the deliverance of the Jews from the massacre plotted by Haman.

Seder: Passover evening meal.

Sheitel: Wig worn by orthodox Jewish women in compliance with the law requiring them to cover their natural hair in public to avoid tempting men.

Shtetl: A small village in czarist Russia inhabited primarily by Jews.

Shul: Synagogue.

Talmud: Voluminous codes of Jewish law representing the commentaries of thousands of Jewish scholars.

Tefillin: Small leather boxes containing parchment scrolls inscribed with Biblical quotations affixed to the foreheads and upper left arms of Jewish males during prayer.

Torah: The first five books of the Old Testament.

Troika: Russian horse-drawn carriage.

Tsimmas: A dessert served as a side dish with Sabbath or holiday meals.

Yeshiva: A school for the study of the Torah.

Yiddishkeit: Jewishness.

Yom Kippur: Day of Atonement. The last of ten days of penitence, beginning with Rosh Hashona.